the Main Characters

OP

350

Edward III
of England

Lionel, Duke of Clarence
(2nd Son)

Edward IV

George, Duke of Clarence

Elizabeth
of York

Edward
Earl of
Warwick

Margaret = Sir Richard Pole
Countess
of Salisbury

Reginald, Cardinal Pole
(d. 1558)

of England = (2) Anne Boleyn

Margaret = James IV of Scotland

James V

Henri II of France
(d. 1559)

Elizabeth I
(d. 1603)

Henry Stuart (2) = Mary, Queen of Scots = (1) Francis
Lord Darnley           (d. 1587)

ELIZABETH II

*The*
*Conspirators*
*and the*
*Crown*

# THE CONSPIRATORS

*Mazye the guene*

# AND THE CROWN

BY *Hugh Ross Williamson*

HAWTHORN BOOKS · NEW YORK

The Library of Congress has catalogued this publication as follows:

Ross Williamson, Hugh,   1901–
    The conspirators and the Crown. ₁1st American ed.₁ New York, Hawthorn Books ₁1959₁
    224 p.  illus.  21 cm.

    1. Mary 1, Queen of England, 1516–1558.  2. Elizabeth, Queen of England, 1533–1603.    1. Title.
DA347.R64                    942.054                    59–6681  ‡
Library of Congress

*To Elizabeth Hare*

# Contents

7

## Contents

8

# Illustrations

9

*The
Conspirators
and the
Crown*

*To the Reader*

This book reads like a novel. But it is not a novel. It is history.

For those interested in plunging into the tragic story of Queen Mary and her relationship with her sister Queen Elizabeth, the story starts here.

For those interested in Mr. Williamson's historical sources, his "A Note on History" appears at the end of the volume.

——THE PUBLISHERS

*ONE*

# Ash
# Wednesday,
# 1554

Aᴛ ᴛwo in the morning of Ash Wednes-
day, 1554, they woke Mary the Queen. A messenger, exhausted with his haste through the bitter storm of the
February night, had brought news to the Palace that the
rebel army had at last managed to cross the Thames and
would be at Hyde Park Corner in two hours.

The Queen heard it with something approaching relief.
At least the matter would now be decided one way or the
other. She looked with some disdain on her younger ladies
who started to sob hysterically as her guard, armed and
carrying their poleaxes, invaded her room for her safety.

"Armed men in a Queen's bedchamber!" . . . "Such a
thing was never heard of!" . . . "We shall all be destroyed!"

She dismissed them all, in that penetrating man's voice
of hers which could almost be mistaken for that of her

13

father, Henry VIII, and told them to attend her in the Presence Chamber in half an hour. Only Mary Browne stayed with her to help her dress—the sturdy maid who had been with her since childhood and who had seen her through far worse moments than this.

"What's your wager this time, Madam?" she asked as soon as they were alone.

Mary the Queen smiled. No one but Mary Browne would have known the right question to ask or would have dared to ask it; for the Queen was a born gambler who, from girlhood, had played for stakes she could not always afford. Sometimes, when she had been a penniless, disinherited princess, forced by her father to become a servant to her young stepsister Elizabeth, she had had nothing to bet on a game of bowls but her breakfast, and more than once she had lost that to Mary Browne. To the maid's discomfort—though secret admiration—she had insisted that she eat it as well as her own. At no time did Mary Tudor default on her debts.

"This isn't your game, Mary. The stakes are too high," said the Queen. "Only my sister Elizabeth can pay *them*. But, not to disappoint you, these earrings against your pomander on what dress I shall choose."

"Your coronation dress, of course," said Mary Browne, holding out her hand for the earrings.

So the little figure of the middle-aged Queen bustled into the Presence Chamber dressed in the magnificent blue velvet and ermine which all London remembered from her coronation procession, less than twenty weeks before. The agitated chatter was stilled to a momentary silence at the rightness of it. But no sooner was she seated than the noise broke out again. One by one her ministers and councilors implored her to take refuge without delay in her fortress of the Tower. She shook her head. The Lord Chancellor—the fifty-seven-year-old Stephen Gardiner, Bishop of Winchester—fell on his knees and besought her to take the boat which he had waiting for her at Whitehall steps to row her to the safety of the City. London's walls were strong; London's gates were shut fast against the rebels, while here, in undefended Westminster . . .

"Do the rebels know, my Lord, where I am—here at Whitehall or at St. James's?"

The Bishop thought not. They had no means of knowing. At least there were no traitors in the Palace.

"Then," said Mary, "they will not know which to attack and they will hardly risk attacking both . . . What time do you sing Mass?"

"At seven, your Grace."

"This Ash Wednesday it would be better at three," said Mary. "I will be in the chapel—here, at Whitehall—at three." Then, as Gardiner bowed to the Tudor obstinacy and left her, she turned to the rest: "You can be assured that I shall set no example of cowardice and, if my captains prove true to their posts, I shall not desert mine."

At four o'clock, when the ceremonies of the Ash Wednesday Mass were ended, she went straight to the most dangerous point in the Palace, the room above the Gatehouse. There she sat quietly, dressed in her coronation robes, but on her forehead no crown but only the black cross, smudged in ashes by Gardiner's thumb as he had said: "Remember, O Man, that dust thou art and to dust thou shall return." Outside she heard the drums beat to arms as her captains disposed their little force of five hundred men for the most effectual defense of the Royal Palaces.

It was, as it happened, not till eleven o'clock in the morning that the rebel troops, impeded by the rain and the mud, arrived with their artillery at the Knight's Bridge, where they divided themselves into three companies. And it was noon before the assault of the Gatehouse of Whitehall commenced. Mary, watching from the Gallery, saw her guards utterly broken and dispersed by the weight of numbers and before the gentlemen-at-arms who were guarding the hall could go to their assistance, the porters in panic had barred the gates, shutting out friend and foe alike.

In vain the gentlemen-at-arms clamored to get out, shouting that it was a scandal to lock the gates on them. Thinking the order had come from the Queen, they begged their commander to go to her with the message that, if only the gates were opened, she should see her enemies fall before her face. Mary agreed at once, asking only that they remain on guard, for, she said, "I have no other defense of my person but you." So they marched, their axes ready, up and down in front of the Gallery, while the main body of fighting surged toward Charing Cross.

She reproached herself for her moment of fear, but almost immediately atoned for it. Edward Courtenay, one of her own cousins, rushed in to her presence with the news that all was lost, that her troops in the Strand were in flight and that the City was on the verge of opening Lud Gate to the rebels. It was not, in fact, true and she sensed it though she did not know then that he was implicated in the insurrection. "That is the foolish notion of those who dare not go near enough to see the truth of the trial," she barked. But, when other fugitives crowded into the Palace, crying: "All is lost! Away! Away! A barge for Her Majesty!" she announced: "I will go myself to the battle and, if need be, die with the brave men who are fighting for me."

That she meant it, no one doubted. They clamored round her, begging her not to take such a risk; but none could prevent her going out from the shelter of the Palace and standing at the head of her gentlemen-at-arms, within easy arquebus-shot of the enemy.

"Where is Lord Pembroke?" she asked.

"Fighting."

"Well, then," she shouted, "all who dare not fight with him may fall to prayers and I warrant we shall hear better news anon." She could not control her sense of relief that, in the sea of treachery surrounding the throne, her commander had stood firm. Then quietly, as if to herself, she added: "God will not deceive me, in Whom my chief trust is."

So she waited, as calmly as if she had been at her prayers, listening to the wild uproar at Charing Cross, where Pembroke, at the head of the cavalry he had kept for the decisive counterattacks, made his last victorious charge.

That evening, after the rebel leaders had been brought in as prisoners and London, after a week of panic, breathed easily once more, she said to Mary Browne, who was helping her take off her coronation dress: "Now it is my sister's turn to pay."

# The
# Lady
# Elizabeth

THAT ELIZABETH had been behind the rebellion, the Queen had no doubt whatever, though the fact that the rebels' avowed object was to dethrone her and set Elizabeth in her place did not particularly weigh with her. She was enough of a politician to know that any discontent in the country would naturally crystallize round her sister. That situation was an axiom of statecraft and she no more blamed Elizabeth for such a phenomenon in the political atmosphere than she would have blamed her for the actual weather. But between an unwilling but inevitable figurehead and an active encourager there was all the difference in the world—the chasm between loyalty and treason; between love and hate.

For long the Queen had refused to believe that her sister was implicated. She had given her the benefit of every doubt till the mounting evidence left her no loophole of comfort. At last she had put her fears to the test on the eve of the rebellion by writing privately in her own hand to Elizabeth, who was at her manor of Ashridge in Berkshire, asking her for safety's sake to come to Court immediately. When Elizabeth not only refused, on the grounds of a pretended illness, but actually prepared to move to Donington Castle which—the Queen knew—the rebels had suggested to her as being more convenient to their plans, Mary realized that further trust was not only useless but dangerous.

Now that the rebellion, after a fortnight's uncertainty about its outcome, was crushed, she summoned Elizabeth to court, this time by a peremptory letter through her Council. An escort was sent to fetch her, accompanied by three doctors, so that the extent of her diplomatic illness could be accurately estimated. Yet Mary could not altogether strangle her affection. In charge of the company sent to make what all understood to be an arrest, she put Elizabeth's great-uncle—uncle to her mother, Anne Boleyn—who besides being her relation was the kindest friend she had in the world. It was a gesture the Queen hoped that her sister would understand.

All her life she had tried to love Elizabeth. When Henry VIII, in the throes of his overmastering lust for the beautiful Anne Boleyn, had divorced Mary's mother to marry her, Mary was seventeen. Suddenly her whole world, the world in which she had been given all the honor belonging to the heir to the throne, crashed about her. At Elizabeth's birth, five months after the marriage, she had not only been degraded in status, forbidden to use the title of Princess and pronounced illegitimate, but she had been forced to submit to every personal indignity that the spite of her stepmother—only eight years her senior—could devise. As far as possible, she had banished the misery of those years into forgetfulness and remembered only the atonement which, at the very end, Anne Boleyn had tried to make.

When, after her three short years of power, Anne lay in prison, awaiting execution for incest and adultery, the one thing which chiefly haunted her was her behavior to Mary. She longed to see her to ask her forgiveness and, when this was denied by the King, she devised a way to make the wronged girl realize the honesty of it. On the day before her death, she took Lady Kingston, the wife of the Governor of the Tower, into her room and, in the presence of her six ladies, made her sit down in the chair of state. Then she fell on her knees before her and, holding up her hands in supplication and with tears in her eyes, said: "As in the presence of God and His angels and as you will answer me before them when we all appear at the Last Judgment, you are to promise me that you will kneel thus to the Lady Mary, my stepdaughter, and, in this manner, beg her forgiveness for the wrongs I have done her; for, till that is done, my conscience will not be quiet."

Lady Kingston gave the message to Mary who, with her lips, sent the dying woman the forgiveness she could not give with her heart. But to invest that pardon with some reality, she determined to be, to the best of her ability, a mother to the helpless baby Elizabeth.

And—to the best of her ability—she had for seventeen difficult years fulfilled that trust.

In the early years, with a procession of four other stepmothers at their father's side and a stepbrother Edward, Prince of Wales, forcing them both into the background, it was comparatively easy; though even then the courtiers were amazed at her temerity in defying prudence and etiquette alike by writing to her father to remind him of his duty to Elizabeth whom, after the death of Anne Boleyn, he had come to hate. But, on the whole, those days when Mary was in her twenties and Elizabeth growing up to a precocious ten, imitating her elder sister's scholarship and skill in music and love of dancing, were happy in memory —and ineradicable.

Things grew more difficult when little Edward became King and Mary, because she refused to change her religion, fell into disgrace, while Elizabeth, who immediately accommodated the authorities, rose to high favor. They were most difficult of all when Edward died and Mary had to fight for her crown against the parvenu millionaires who had used him as a tool for making their fortunes by plundering the property of the Church and feared lest she, as Queen, should make them disgorge their gains. Though she could not even then be sure that Elizabeth, changed by her taste of power, was not secretly on their side, she made a supreme effort to bind her to hers by love. When she had won her throne from Lady Jane Grey and entered London in triumph, she gave Elizabeth the place of honor at her side. She was scrupulous never to appear in public or to dine publicly without her. She held her hand and showed her, almost ostentatiously, every mark of favor to still the gossips who argued, logically enough, that since Mary was now indubitably acknowledged the legitimate heir of Henry VIII by the laws of State and Church alike and admitted to be so by the whole of Europe, of necessity Elizabeth was technically a bastard. At Mary's crowning, Elizabeth still held the place of honor, with the implication that, whatever her birth, she was heir to the throne.

In private, the Queen gave her sister not only tokens of affection but the affection itself that she had never withheld. Yet, in spite of it all, she knew Elizabeth no longer returned it. Outwardly, of course, it was not apparent. Elizabeth remained at twenty the vivacious, amusing, talented child she had always been—Mary, at thirty-seven, still regarded her as a child—combining expressions of affection with marks of deference. Yet now it rang false and when she asked the Queen's permission to withdraw from court to her house in the country, Mary sensed that a chapter in their lives was closed and dreaded the opening of a new one.

Impulsively, at their parting, she had given her a ring.

"Take this, Bess."

Elizabeth had looked at it in surprise: "But this is one of your mother's rings, Mary."

"Then you know how I value it."

"But I cannot——"

"Bess," Mary had said as she kissed her, "who knows what these times will do to us? Keep it till you need me desperately. Then you can send it back."

When the news arrived at Court that the Princess Elizabeth was pronounced well enough to travel and was approaching London in easy stages not exceeding eight miles a day, the Queen said to Mary Browne: "My sister has decided to meet her debts. I think her first payment will be a ring."

Elizabeth had disliked Mary for as long as she could remember. As a child, fastidious and withdrawn into herself, she had instinctively avoided, whenever she could, the caresses of the melancholy-faced woman with the loud

23

voice and peering, short-sighted eyes who bustled round her like a maternal hen. As she grew older and understood the implications of their relationship, she controlled herself to an appearance of response. Very early in life she learnt the art of dissimulation and saw to it that her stepsister had no clue to her real feelings. She accepted Mary's gifts with a charming show of gratitude; she adopted Mary's hobbies and enthusiasms; and, when she had a household of her own she was scrupulous to visit and to entertain Mary and to correspond with her in terms of sisterly affection.

Yet, to herself, she lived in a secret world where she was by right a Queen and Mary but the dull stepsister who was her servant. In this world it was a memorable date when she found she was actually taller than Mary: more memorable the day when she realized that her fresh beauty, her golden hair and olive skin, brought men's eyes in her direction and that her elegance accentuated Mary's dumpy, homely figure. She loved to look at her own slim, exquisite hands which she had inherited from her mother and contrast them with her sister's thick, capable ones which Mary had only too obviously inherited from her father.

Her mother's blood was strong in her. Even the remembrance of Anne Boleyn's end and the Court gossip about her lovers, which Elizabeth pretended not to hear, acted not as a deterrent but as a spur. She would wipe out the memory of it and avenge her mother in her own way. She would love passionately, exquisitely, capriciously, where and when she chose and, when she tired of her lovers, would send them to death or oblivion. At fifteen, she had her first love affair with the forty-year-old Admiral of England, who was sent to the block for it when it was discovered. Those who diagnosed her subsequent illness in terms of sorrow and strain were altogether too simple in their estimate of her reactions. After this experience, contempt was added to the emotions with which she regarded Mary. After all, Mary, with her piety and good works, really knew nothing of life . . . Elizabeth, in her teens, was actually older and more experienced than Mary at thirty-two . . .

As long as Edward VI lived, her Narcissus-world of imaginings remained unshattered. She was his favorite sister and even though, in a boyish way, he had disapproved slightly of her affair with the Admiral, he disapproved far more strongly of Mary for refusing to deny her religion at his request. Elizabeth regarded her young brother's reign as a period during which she would gradually assert her claim to be the royal darling of the country and the domestic power behind the throne, while Mary, by her obstinate honesty in religious matters, would eventually land herself in prison. And as Edward was delicate, the reign might not last too long; just long enough to leave the way unquestionably clear for herself to succeed him as Queen . . .

Then, suddenly, the breath of reality scattered the rose-mist of dreams. Unexpectedly, Edward died before he reached the age of sixteen and, in spite of the intrigues of the new nobility to place Lady Jane Grey, their tool, on the throne, the country was so completely behind Mary that that first attempt at Protestant rebellion was snuffed out almost before it was alight. Elizabeth, immediately adapting herself to the changed circumstances, went to Court to bask in her sister's unsuspecting affection. The coronation was, from her point of view, an unqualified success. She noticed triumphantly how spectators' eyes strayed from the Queen to her.

Then Mary in her foolishness committed two actions which destroyed the possibility of even an appearance of friendship. She had her legitimacy reaffirmed by Act of Parliament and she announced that she intended to marry Philip of Spain. The first meant that Elizabeth's bastardy was established beyond argument: the second meant that, illegitimate or not, Elizabeth could now not only head a party in the country—simple, loyal men whom it would be easy to rouse to fear at the prospect of a foreign king—but could also rely on France, fearing the power of an Anglo-Spanish alliance, to finance and foment any possible discontent. So she ostentatiously withdrew from Court, hardly daring to look Mary in the face lest the Queen should see the hatred in her eyes or read the treason in her heart.

Nor, she was sure, had she been successful in masking them. To her surprise and chagrin, Mary had given her a ring, accompanied by strange words which suggested that she had read her thoughts. And when, on the eve of the rebellion, Mary sent for her to return to the Palace, she knew that the Queen knew. She had indeed disobeyed the summons, feigning illness to gain the precious time needed to know whether or not the rebellion would succeed. But now, with the rebels defeated and captured; with—she feared—her correspondence with the French Ambassador discovered; with a command, backed by force, which could not be disobeyed, she saw no escape from Mary's justice. When, under the eyes of her great-uncle and the doctors, she entered the litter which had been sent to convey her to London, there was no need for further feigning. She was really ill.

*THREE*

# Three
# Spanish
# Matters

T HE SPANISH Ambassador, Simon Renard, craved an audience of the Queen. He found her, when he entered, gazing intently at a miniature of Philip of Spain. For a moment he supposed it was a deliberate affectation. Though he was the most skilled of diplomats, he was continually baffled to know whether Mary's apparent simplicity was a foolish, insular honesty or a subtlety as wary as his own. A glance at her face made him decide that, on this occasion, he had to deal with a middle-aged woman in love with love—or with youth.

"This portrait," she said, "is it more like the Prince than the others?"

Renard looked at it and noticed that Philip's thick, sensual lips and heavy-lidded, disdainful eyes had been minimized by the artist. In fact, he hardly recognized the Prince. "A most excellent likeness," he said.

"His hair is as golden as that?"

"To a shade."

"He looks so young. I still fear, Señor, that when he comes he will think me old."

Renard, who knew that the dissolute, twenty-six-year-old Philip, already a widower, privately referred to Mary, eleven years his senior as "our well-beloved aunt," hastened to assure her that such a thing was unthinkable. "Nor, Highness, for all his glow of youth will you find in him the imperfections of the young. In his character he is so settled that he has all the—how can I put it?—all the *safe* virtues of a husband of fifty."

"Of fifty?" said Mary. "His father is only fifty-four in a fortnight."

"Yes, Highness." Renard took refuge in silence. He no longer pretended to have a clue to Mary's mind.

"I find it easy to remember the Emperor's birthday," Mary added. "It is two days after mine."

It is necessary for a diplomat to live in the present; but not even the acutest diplomat can be sure where other people are living. For months Renard had thought of nothing but this coming marriage between Philip and Mary. Obviously—and the recent rebellion, which had had as its rallying-cry: "No Spanish marriage," had proved it—no other topic approached it in importance. But Mary was, for the moment, living in the far past, the golden moments of her childhood before the gray misery of her father's divorce had clouded the sun.

She was six when, on a summer day, she had been brought to Greenwich and stood with her mother, Queen Catherine of Aragon, at the garden door of the palace and watched her father bring with him from the Royal Barge which had drawn up at the water-steps, her cousin, the

Emperor Charles V, King of Spain and the Netherlands, a pale, reserved young man of twenty-two, who kissed her hand and explained that he was going to be her husband. She had liked him immediately. Observant courtiers might notice that his legs were too short for his body, which was bowed from over-exercise on horseback; that his lower jaw was so undershot that his teeth did not meet; that he spoke with a lisping stammer and that the eyes, light blue and protuberant in the long, pallid face, were as cold and impassive as a mask. But Charles, even then, had a way with children. Also, he was genuinely fond of his aunt, Catherine of Aragon, whose son-in-law he was now to be. And Mary, in the way that children have, sensed the affection and overlooked the appearance.

During the five weeks Charles was in England, she had come to think of herself as his Empress, to the amusement of her ladies; and at the end of the visit she curtsied to him with a grave solemnity when, at Windsor, he had signed the matrimonial treaty by which he pledged himself to marry her as soon as she was twelve.

So, for the next three years, the little girl dreamt of her destiny and studied, under her Spanish tutor, to prepare herself for it. She imagined herself in love. Perhaps she really was in love. At least she understood what jealousy was when she heard her ladies discussing the possibility of Charles having to make a political marriage elsewhere. When she was nine, she sent Charles one of her own rings —an emerald, which is the color of constancy and which, so they say, pales in its vivid green if the heart of the betrothed swerves from the affianced. The English Ambassador presented it to the Emperor with the message she had herself composed: "Her Grace hath devised this token for a better knowledge to be had whether His Majesty doth keep constant to her, as with God's grace she will to him."

Charles put the ring on his little finger, forced it down as far as it would go and instructed the Ambassador to report that "he would wear it for the sake of the Princess."

But within a year he had married Isabella, the beautiful Princess of Portugal, and Mary had received sorrow's first blow. The girl of ten, the Court noticed, went white and faint with the hurt of it. They attributed it to a fantasy of jealousy, encouraged by the maids-of-honor's chatter about love.

But they were wrong. The very young are less equipped than the old only to mask misery, not to feel it. Now, twenty-seven years later, the memory of it could still move her. Even her father's creation of her as Princess of Wales with her own Court at Ludlow had been an excitement which was no consolation.

And now she was to marry the son of Charles and Isabella, because Charles wished it. Seldom had Renard made a greater miscalculation than when he had seen in her a middle-aged woman doting on the picture of a young lover. She was, in fact, searching Philip's countenance to see how much of his mother there was in him and she was looking with the eyes of the jilted child who had not been able, for weeks, to trust herself to ask about her rival.

"The Prince's chin juts out less than his father's," she said.

"Both have an admirable determination," said Renard.

"When does he set sail?"

This was the opening the Ambassador had been waiting for and he decided that it was the moment to strike.

"He can venture, Highness, only when it is safe."

"Safe? Does he fear the spring storms?"

"I was not meaning the sea but the land. This land. It was for this I craved audience with Your Majesty. I wish to be able to assure Prince Philip and the Emperor that the Lady Elizabeth will be brought to trial and execution before he arrives for his marriage to Your Majesty."

Mary asked incredulously: "Is that a condition the Emperor has made?"

"Not formally, Madame. But, informally, I can assure you that it will be so."

The Queen stiffened. "In England, Señor, we do not condemn to death those who have not committed open acts of treason. All that I can say is that I and my council are laboring to discover the truth about my sister's practices. But we have no proof."

"If I may venture, Madame, it is common knowledge that, at the very least, the Princess your sister gave the rebellion her consent by silence."

"Silence, Señor, is not high treason."

The Ambassador, pulling at his beard, accepted the reproof.

"You know, Madame, that I should never presume to tender advice on the matter of your own laws. But in the duty I owe to my master the Emperor Charles and to his son Prince Philip, I have been bound to report that the state of England is such that it would be unsafe for the Prince to venture his person here until the head of rebellion is cut off."

"And their answer?"

"With infinite regret, I have to inform Your Majesty that Prince Philip will not come to England while the Princess Elizabeth lives."

Renard, bowing himself out, noticed with satisfaction that, even before the door closed, the Queen had taken up once more the miniature of her bridegroom-to-be and was studying his features.

When Renard had gone, the Queen sent for her Lord Chancellor.

She had never wholly trusted Stephen Gardiner, for in her father's reign he had been one of those who had connived at the King's proceedings. He had been Wolsey's secretary. He had been the enemy of her mother and the opponent of the martyred Thomas More. Nevertheless she was convinced that he had been honest in his belief that it was possible to remain a Catholic and deny the Pope's supremacy: and that his five years in the Tower during the Protestant ascendancy in Edward VI's reign had more than convinced him of his error of judgment. Fanatical in defense of every Catholic dogma, and especially of the Blessed Sacrament, he had discovered too late that without the Pope's protection, the very fundamentals of the Faith were in jeopardy.

When Mary had released him from prison and restored him to his See of Winchester, he had as a matter of fact determined to atone for his mistake by ensuring that religion was not again imperiled. Witty, choleric, unafraid of anyone on earth and inflexible of purpose, he was now, in his fifty-seventh year (although, because of the rigors of his long imprisonment, seeming older), the terror of heretics. On the other hand, English of the English, he also disliked the Spanish marriage and lost no opportunity of saying so. But above all, as a great lawyer, accustomed to dealing with evidence, he had no shadow of doubt of Elizabeth's guilt in the rebellion and against her he was implacable.

Now, summoned to Mary's presence, he told the Queen bluntly: "As long as Elizabeth lives, there is no hope of the

"She remembered her father . . . in the throes of his lust . . ."
*(The Hans Holbein portrait of Henry VIII)*

"—who had divorced
her mother—
Catherine of Aragon—

"—for the beautiful
Anne Boleyn. . . ."

kingdom being tranquilized and if everyone, Madame, went to work as roundly as we, your Councilors, are trying to do, things would be better."

"My Lord Bishop," said Mary quietly, "you have forgotten your charity."

"And you, Madame," retorted Gardiner, "are in danger of forgetting the cause of our holy religion which you are putting in jeopardy by a misguided clemency."

He proceeded to tell her how, that very morning, a crowd of some thousand Londoners were standing near an empty house in Aldersgate Street, listening to a strange supernatural voice which had become the talk of the city. Whenever the crowd shouted: "God save Queen Mary!" there was silence, but when they cried "God save the Lady Elizabeth!" the voice replied: "So be it," and if they asked "What is the Mass?" it answered: "Idolatry!" The Council had sent down officers to quiet the spirit by the practical means of pulling down the wall and had discovered there a girl who confessed that she had been hired by Elizabeth's sympathizers to excite the mob.

"You cannot blame my sister for that, even if it was done in her name," Mary answered, "and since thousands saw the truth discovered, it may teach them to be less credulous in future."

Gardiner, realizing that argument was useless, contented himself with remarking: "They will always find some excuse to cry your sister's name till you take it from them. Pray God you will before it is too late."

"I will not be guilty," said the Queen, "of my sister's blood."

"Guilty of *that?* Blood ten times forfeit for treason! Besides, Madame," he shot at her, as he bowed to take his leave, "you and I know what we know."

33

# FOUR

# Elizabeth
# Comes to
# London

Elizabeth arrived at Highgate nine days after she set out from Ashridge. With the aid of her doctors she had by this time mastered her illness and had determined to enter the capital in state. In order that the news of her impending progress should have time to spread to all Londoners, she had a slight relapse which enabled her to spend forty-eight hours with her Highgate host. She needed the time, also, to ensure that sufficient of her own gentlemen could ride in to attend her and to arouse Mary's suspicions sufficiently to send out a Royal escort which she could use to enhance the splendor of the occasion.

On Wednesday, February 21, exactly a fortnight after the crushing of the insurrection, she started the last stage of her journey to Westminster. Carefully dressed in white, as an indication of innocence, she lay propped up in a litter with the curtain drawn back and smiled wanly at the crowds which lined the way from Highgate to Smithfield. Round her, as a guard of honor, rode a hundred of her gentlemen, magnificent in velvet coats of all colors. Behind them marched a hundred of the Queen's guard, in their livery of scarlet and black.

At Smithfield the crowd became denser. The air here was foul with the smell of death, for at door after door dangled the bodies of men of the train-bands who, a fortnight before, had deserted the Queen's standard. As the procession passed up Fleet Street to Temple Bar, Elizabeth braced herself for the sight which she knew was awaiting her there—the heads of some of the rebel leaders, grinning ghastly on poles. But the physical shock of it, prepared for, was less, when it came, than the one thing she had not reckoned with—the complete silence of the onlookers. Not a cheer, not a solitary shout of "God save the Lady Elizabeth," was raised to give her courage. There were looks of sympathy; there were—or so she imagined—even tears here and there; there was an inscrutable anger; but there was no welcome. The clatter of the horses' hooves and the steady tread of the Queen's guard drowned even the strained whispers. The stillness made it seem a funeral procession: a funeral procession with herself the living corpse. Only by a supreme effort of will did she refrain from ordering that the curtains of the litter should be drawn and, instead, continued, like a great white doll with a carved smile, to acknowledge the citizens who did not or dared not acknowledge her.

The Lord Chamberlain met her at the garden-gate of Whitehall and, with every appearance of deference, conducted her to the apartments which had been prepared for her. They were in a distant part of the palace and were inaccessible without passing the ordinary palace guard. Of the Queen there was no sign; nor was there any message from her.

"My sister . . . ?"

"Her Majesty is occupied with business."

For the next twenty-three days she asked that question and received that answer.

On the twenty-fourth day, the eve of Palm Sunday, she sent Mary back her ring.

That day, her position, she thought, was desperate. Mary had suddenly ordered her to the Tower and all her calculations of safety vanished when the Lord Chamberlain came to tell her that her barge was waiting to take her there. For the last three weeks, while the examinations and trials of the rebels were proceeding, she had, despite her danger, clung to the hope that ultimately she was safe because of a lack of evidence against her. Now, with Traitor's Gate at the end of a short river journey, she wondered desperately how much her sister knew. If the plot itself had miscarried, what could not go wrong?

The plan had seemed so certain. There were to be four risings, timed simultaneously. In Wales, the leader was Sir James Croft, the Controller of her Household who, in her brother's reign, had been Lord Deputy of Ireland—a man apt for both war and intrigue. In Devon, the leader was her cousin Edward Courtenay, young, charming, weak and dissolute, to whom she was to be married when she was proclaimed Queen—an English King and Queen of Hearts instead of the Spanish Philip and the half-Spanish Mary. In Leicestershire, the Duke of Suffolk, father of Lady Jane Grey, was in command and Elizabeth herself was to leave Ashridge (where, a mere thirty-three miles from London, she would have been in danger of capture) for the safety of Donington Castle, near Suffolk's head-quarters. In Kent, Sir Thomas Wyatt, soldier-son of the poet who had been one of her mother's lovers, was to lead the attack.

The rebellion was to take place in the spring, by which time it was calculated that the country as a whole would, by unceasing propaganda, have been goaded into fury against the proposed "Spanish marriage," and would rise spontaneously behind the insurgents. The King of France, to whom the Anglo-Spanish alliance was indeed anathema, would provide all the aid he could—certainly financial, possibly, in the last resort, military—through his Ambassador, de Noailles, who, to facilitate access to Elizabeth, had married one of her maids-of-honor. Through him, Elizabeth had supplied the King with a copy of the letter she had written to Mary, pleading sickness as an excuse for not leaving Ashridge, so that she could in fact escape to the safety of Donington Castle. Henri II would understand the implication. In things not concerning France she had used as her personal link with the conspirators her trusted cousin-by-marriage, Sir Francis Knollys.

Altogether the plan had seemed certain of success when, through the sagacity of Gardiner and the instability of Courtenay, it was discovered. Wyatt had thus been forced to make his attack before he was fully prepared and Suffolk and Croft were arrested before they could rise at all. Courtenay, to save himself from suspicion, made a show of fighting against Wyatt when he made his assault on London, though this gesture merely postponed his arrest. And now Elizabeth herself had been ordered to join the other prisoners in the Tower where she would, she knew, be examined by Gardiner and the Lords of the Council. Her one consolation was that Knollys, the only man who could utterly incriminate her—and who knew what even the bravest might be brought to say under torture?—had managed to escape to the Continent; her fear was that another member of her household, Sir William Saintlow, who had been indiscreet enough to join Wyatt in making a public proclamation at Tunbridge, might be prevailed on to tell what he knew. And could she trust Croft, who had made the arrangements for the fortification of Donington Castle?

Suddenly she was terrified. An examination by Gardiner, implacable and unimpressed by her charm, was the road to death. At all costs, before the gates of the Tower closed on her, she must see Mary. Whatever policy might demand or evidence justify, sister would not kill sister. She remembered how, five years ago, her lover, the Admiral, had been condemned to death by his brother, the Protector Somerset, and how Somerset had told her, when it was too late, that the fratricide would have been impossible had he actually spoken to him face to face. So she must stand face to face with Mary. And Mary, after all, had promised it. That was the meaning of the ring. The ring was the guarantee that she would not be condemned unheard. She would keep Mary to her word—Mary who had taught her, in the far-off days when both were under their father's displeasure and she had broken a childish promise, of how King John of France had said when he voluntarily returned to captivity in England: "A King's word is more than another man's oath."

She turned to the Lord Chamberlain: "If my sister will not see me before you take me to the Tower, at least you will let me write to her?"

"I will do more, Your Grace," he answered. "As I am a true man I will myself deliver your letter to the Queen."

39

She settled down to write, in her exquisite hand, carefully and slowly—for if she took long enough she would miss the tide and that would mean at least a day's respite from the Tower—"If any ever did try this old saying, that 'a King's word was more than another man's oath' I most humbly beseech Your Majesty to verify it to me and to remember your last promise and my last demand—that I be not condemned without answer and due proof, which it seems that I now am; for, without cause proved, I am by your council from you commanded to go to the Tower. I protest before God (who shall judge my truth, whatsoever malice shall devise) that I never practised, counselled nor consented to anything that might be prejudicial to your person any way or dangerous to the state by any means."

That, she decided, was true enough. No one had suggested killing Mary and what was dangerous to the state was a matter of opinion. As far as she was concerned the Spanish marriage would be much more dangerous than the rule of herself and Courtenay.

"And therefore," she continued, "I humbly beseech Your Majesty to let me answer afore yourself and not suffer me to trust to your councillors—yea, and that afore I go to the Tower, if it be possible; if not, before I be further condemned. Let conscience move Your Highness to pardon this my boldness, which innocency procures me to do, together with the hope of your natural kindness, which I trust will not see me cast away without desert. I have heard of many in my time cast away for want of coming to the presence of their prince; and in late days I heard my lord of Somerset say that, if his brother had been suffered to speak to him, he had never suffered; but persuasions were made to him so great he was brought to the belief that he could not live safely if the Admiral lived, and that made him give consent to his death. Though these persons are not to be compared to Your Majesty, yet I pray God that like evil persuasions persuade not one sister against the other.

"Therefore, once again, kneeling with humbleness of heart because I am not suffered to bow the knees of my body, I humbly crave to speak with Your Highness, which I would not be so bold as to desire if I knew not myself most clear as I know myself most true."

But was she clear? She had heard the persistent rumor that Wyatt's letters to her had been discovered and that the copy of her letter sent to the French King had been intercepted. As both these were harmless, it might be prudent to mention them. She knew there were no letters from herself to Wyatt, since she had been careful to send only verbal messages by Knollys; and the copy of her letter, with which she had left de Noailles to deal, was not, in fact, to Henri II.

"And as for the traitor Wyatt," she concluded with a fine flourish, "he might peradventure write me a letter, but on my faith I never received any from him. And as for the copy of the letter sent to the French King, I pray God confound me eternally if I ever sent him word, message, token or letter, by any means; and to this truth I will stand to my death.

"Your Highness's most faithful subject that hath been from the beginning and will be to my end,

Elizabeth."

She read it over carefully and added a postscript: "I humbly crave but only one word of answer from yourself."

When she had sealed it, she took off Mary's ring and gave it, with the letter, to the Lord Chamberlain: "If you will indeed do me, my Lord, the service you promised, you will deliver both these to the Queen, my sister."

Next morning, as Mary did not reply, she was taken to the Tower. On her way to the barge, walking through the Queen's Garden, she looked up at the window of her sister's apartments in the hope of seeing her. Perhaps she would at least give an answering nod. But there was no one there. Mary was walking in the Palm Sunday procession at Westminster Abbey; and as, in spite of the rain, the London crowds had thronged to see the Royal appearance, Elizabeth had to leave the Palace, not only without seeing Mary but without seeing anyone except those who were guarding her.

At the Watergate of the Tower, however, she found an audience, even it it was only a small and official one. As she stepped ashore she raised her eyes to Heaven and announced in a voice loud enough for all to hear: "Here lands as true a subject, being prisoner, as ever landed at these stairs. Before Thee, O God, I speak it, having no other friend but Thee alone."

Then, as if recollecting the presence of the soldiers and the warders and their families, she added: "I pray you all, good friends and fellows, bear me witness that I come no traitor but as true a woman to the Queen's Majesty as any now living."

Having so delivered herself, she sat down on a cold, wet stone, just outside the Gate.

"Madame," said the Lieutenant of the Tower, "you had best come in out of the rain, for you sit unwholesomely."

"Better sit here than in a worse place," she retorted. "God knows, but I do not, where you will lead me."

But there was no help for it. At last she had to enter the Tower, where they had killed her mother.

Her examination a week later by Gardiner and the other Councilors bristled with new dangers. For one thing, the Lord Chancellor was incensed at what he considered the Queen's blindness. On Good Friday, merely because it was Good Friday, Mary had insisted on giving a free pardon to eight men undoubtedly implicated in the rebellion; and the eight included courtiers of such eminence as the Marquis of Northampton and Lord Cobham.

This fatal mercy reinforced what Gardiner already realized—that Mary would not rid herself of Elizabeth unless the proofs were of such a nature that acquittal was impossible. To obtain such proofs he had labored to the best of his ability. He had three dispatches of de Noailles to the French King which made it quite clear that the sole object of the conspiracy was to set Elizabeth on the throne. He had the copy of her letter sent to Henri II. He had the oath of the Duke of Suffolk (who, having been already executed, could not retract it) that Elizabeth was the pivot of the insurgents' plans. Wyatt had admitted his correspondence with Elizabeth and Gardiner had, in fact, two of his letters—the first urging her to move to Donington Castle, the second announcing his capture of Southwark. Sir James Croft had confessed that he had conferred with her and "solicited her to retire to Donington" and others had given evidence of preparing it as a fortress.

It was, therefore, to the last degree unfortunate that, when Gardiner asked her her motives in preparing to move to Donington Castle, she assumed an air of injured innocence and said that she did not recollect that she possessed such a property. When Sir James Croft was brought in to confront her she experienced a moment of panic before, with a cynical disregard of her first answer, she could control herself sufficiently to say: "As touching my removal to Donington, my officers and you, Sir James Croft, being then present, can well testify whether any rash or unbecoming word did then pass my lips, which might not well have become a faithful and loyal subject."

Croft, confused, fell on his knees and answered: "I am heartily sorry to be brought in this day as a witness against Your Grace; but I take God to my record that I never knew anything of you worthy the least suspicion."

She looked at him keenly. As he returned her gaze without wavering, she judged that, apart from the arrangements at Donington, he had said nothing to incriminate her; and that he was, in fact, trying to tell her that she could continue to protest her innocence now that her original lie about Donington had been admitted. She turned to the Lords of the Council and assumed an indignation which soothed her fear: "My lords, I think you do me wrong in examining every mean prisoner against me. If they have done evil, let them answer for it; but do not, I pray you, join me with them. As regards my removal from Ashridge to Donington, I now remember that my officers and you, Sir James Croft, did speak about it. But what has that to do with the matter? May I not, my lords, go to whichever of my houses I choose, whenever I choose?"

Gardiner remained silent, but another Councilor, voicing the majority, assured her that she could and apologized for troubling her about irrelevancies. Nor was she troubled again.

But in the ensuing days of silence, fear once more took possession of her, and, at her nadir, she wrote another letter to Mary, making her last request—that she might, like her mother, have her head cut off with a sword instead of an axe and that, if she were marked to die, an expert executioner should once more be brought over from France.

# FIVE

# The
# Tardy
# Bridegroom

MARY NEEDED all her courage. Through-
out Eastertide she lived in daily fear of assassination. The
trials of the rebels and the restored ceremonies of the
Church provided a double focus for sedition. Rumors
of a new rebellion were spread everywhere. In the streets,
even the children played the game of "Wyatt and the
Spaniards," and the boy who played Philip was hanged in
fun till he was almost dead in fact—"would bear," as the
French Ambassador put it, "the marks for many a day."
Into the palace were thrown obscene pamphlets and a
dead cat dressed in Mass vestments with its head tonsured.
A gun was fired at a preacher at St. Paul's Cross and during a procession a knife-attack was made on the priest
bearing the Monstrance.

The Council, fearing an attempt on the Queen, doubled
the guards in the Presence Chamber and so curtailed audi-

47

ences that no lord, whatever his rank, might come into the presence attended by more than one person.

Though Mary's spirit was untamed, her weak body could no longer match it. No less than her Councilors, her physicians, George Owen and Thomas Wendy, who had attended her father and known her from childhood, were concerned for her life; but she insisted on keeping on her feet to participate in the services of Easter Week. Even when they were over, on the morrow of Low Sunday, a day of relentless wind and storm, she attended Westminster Abbey in state to assist at the Mass of the Holy Ghost—the traditional "Red Mass" which, in Catholic England, had always preceded the opening of Parliament to implore on its deliberations the light and wisdom of the Holy Spirit. But, after that, she could do no more. She was now palpably too ill to open Parliament itself later in the day. Gardiner, as Lord Chancellor, performed the ceremony for her and outlined the business of the session —the confirmation of the articles of her marriage to Philip, the succession and the measures to be taken for the restoration of religion.

On the first matter, there was no difficulty; on the second, no satisfaction. There was no opposition to her marriage; there was every opposition to the legal disinheriting of Elizabeth. Her wishes about the heir-presumptive were well enough known. The very vehemence with which she had stated it, both in the previous Parliament and to her Lords of the Council, was the measure of her disappointment. Elizabeth, she had said, should never reign in England with her consent. It was a matter of conscience, quite apart from the genealogical fact that Mary Queen of Scots was her true and legitimate successor. Elizabeth was a bastard, daughter of an infamous woman who had been the cause of all the alterations and troubles in the realm. She was a heretic, having none but secret or open heretics in her service, and, should she become Queen, the ruin of the Faith would continue. She was a hypocrite and, even should she profess Catholicism, Mary could never trust her . . . These things the Queen had said before Wyatt's rebellion. Now she knew, as the Council knew, that Elizabeth was an active traitor. But Parliament would not disinherit her. And Mary's knowledge of the reason for this added to the burden of her misery.

That reason was the third matter under discussion. Had Mary consented to promise that she would make no attempt to restore to the Church the lands that had been taken from it, she could immediately have had her way about her sister. She was under no illusions about that. But, because she considered it a treason to God, she could not do it; and because she would not do it the Lords of the Council—every one of whom, except Gardiner, were in possession of fortunes pillaged from the Church—kept Elizabeth as a card to play against her. Protestant support of Elizabeth, Mary understood; French support, she assumed; but the secret support of those who called themselves Catholic but preferred Mammon to God sent ice to her heart. Far easier to pardon the tonsured cat than the gesture of Russell who threw his rosary in the fire saying that, much as he loved it, he loved his sweet Abbey of Woburn more. He spoke for them all. Yet these men were necessary to her and to England. Without them she could not rule. She must accept their corruption and their power a little longer. Until Philip arrived. The marriage with Philip would transform the scene and accomplish what

49

persuasion and honesty could not. But from Philip she had still received no word . . .

His father, indeed, had sent her a jewel, a great green emerald, which she had shown with delight to her ladies. The younger ones thought her delight excessive; but the older, who knew what the emerald signified between her and Charles, understood. As soon as Parliament had ratified her marriage, she made that decision the excuse, ill as she still was, to write to Philip with the news. The letter stirred him at last to the belated courtesy of a communication. With his letter, he sent a ring, a great diamond set in a rose, which his father had once given to his mother. She saw Charles in this, too, and accepted the ring as if it had been the one she should have had before Philip was born. For that reason, not because Philip had sent it, she valued it above the additional presents from Charles himself— many rare jewels and exquisite tapestries.

On her side she ordered preparations to be made. A suit of gold and a suit of silver tissue for Philip were put in hand. Magnificent embroideries of the arms and devices of England and Spain were commissioned for the hangings of the nuptial bed. And forty young and handsome gentlemen, magnificently attired, were sent to Spain to accompany the bridegroom across the sea.

No dreams of the future, however, could dispel the gray reality of the present. Rebellion still ruled. Though Wyatt was executed and his head set on a pole at St. James's as a warning to traitors, the rumor was set about that on the scaffold he had exonerated Elizabeth. It was quite false and rumor-mongers, when discovered, were set in the pillory; but, necessarily, it was widely believed. Another of the conspirators was acquitted, in defiance of the evidence, by a London jury. A few days later Wyatt's head was stolen—a feat which argued considerable complicity.

At this point—it was late in April—Mary was so ill that Gardiner, fearing that she might die, determined that Elizabeth should die first. On his own responsibility, he sent a Privy Council warrant to the Lieutenant of the Tower ordering her execution. But the Lieutenant, perturbed by the absence of the Queen's signature, refused to proceed in so grave a constitutional matter until he had had direct communication with her on the matter. The necessary delay, until Mary had recovered sufficiently to deal with it, not only saved Elizabeth's life but created in Mary, when she heard of it, an immediate revulsion in her favor. Bastard, traitor, heretic and hypocrite, Bess might be: but nothing could obliterate the ties of the past . . .

At the edge of death which, cheated, had become the threshold of a new happiness and the prologue to an age of restoration and hope, Mary saw in a necessity of political wisdom nothing but a personal blood-guiltiness and, seeing, recoiled from it in horror. The ruler was lost in the woman. She stormed at Gardiner, ostentatiously restored Elizabeth's portrait to a place of honor in the Palace, pardoned Sir James Croft and sent Sir Henry Bedingfield, a forty-three-year-old Norfolk gentleman of meticulous probity, with a hundred men-at-arms to guard Elizabeth from danger in the Tower.

In the circumstances, it was natural enough for Elizabeth to mistake Mary's action and, when she first saw Bedingfield and his blue-coats march into the inner court, to assume that they had come to supervise her execution. In terror she asked whether Lady Jane Grey's scaffold on the Green had been dismantled. The Lieutenant of the

Tower put her quickly at ease. He explained that she had
no cause for alarm; that Bedingfield had come to guarantee her safety; that she could now have the liberty of four
rooms for herself and her attendants into which no one
was to come but her own servants and those of the Queen;
that she was free to walk in the garden in the morning and
the afternoon and, whenever she pleased, in the great
chamber next to her own apartments; and that, as soon as
it could be arranged, she would leave the Tower for the
pleasant palace of Woodstock.

Had the Queen sent any special message to her? None.
How was she? She had been very ill but was now recovered. Yesterday she had made her first appearance in public for a month. As it was Rogation-tide, she had gone in
procession, with four bishops and her heralds and ser-
geants-at-arms, to her chapels in the fields. Mass was sung
at St. Giles-in-the-Fields and at St. Martin-in-the-Fields
and a third, where a sermon was preached, at St. Margaret's in Westminster. At Westminster they had made
good cheer and then gone back to St. James's through the
Park, beating the bounds of it. And now? Today Her
Majesty was resting. Tomorrow she was to dissolve the
Parliament . . .

Mary had indeed gone a-Maying in her own way. The
loveliness of those first days of May saw the cloud lift
from her spirit as pain had from her body and, as if to
confirm her in her sudden happiness, the Commons, when
she went to the House for the dissolution, cheered her to
the echo in unmistakable affection and loyalty, while
from the Lords many came to seek her out to assure her of
their personal fidelity, however they might differ in their
opinions. It was, perhaps, a tribute to her gallantry
throughout those three months since Wyatt had invaded

London—a crisis which might have tested the resources of an experienced King. Whatever the motive, she was for that moment an English monarch superbly at one with her counselors and Renard, in despair of ever understanding the national temperament, wrote home to Spain that "the changeableness of these people is unbelievable!"

A week after Elizabeth set out for Woodstock, Mary went to Windsor to await there, in the serenity of a perfect English countryside flowering to summer, the arrival from her mother's country of the man who would bring her a late and unlooked-for happiness.

But still Philip delayed.

# *Wedding at Winchester*

JUNE HAD gone and half July before Philip's ships were sighted off the Needles. Late it might be, but at least the day was propitious. It was July 19 and Renard who, for the last month, had had his diplomacy strained to distraction, made the most of it. "Sire," he wrote to the Emperor, "a year ago this very day the Queen was proclaimed Queen of England." Mary, who needed no reminder of the anniversary, accepted it as an omen with the rest, and made preparations to leave Farnham Castle where, a day's ride from Winchester, she had been staying as Gardiner's guest. In less than a week now she would be married. In the Cathedral of Winchester, ancient capital of England, on the Feast of St. James, patron saint of Spain, she would become Philip's wife. Charles's son would put on her finger that plain gold ring which, despite her Councilors' preference for a richly jeweled one, she had insisted on, because, she said, "maids were so married in old time and I will be wedded with a plain hoop of gold like any other maiden." It was the one permitted concession to the personal. Next Wednesday, the eyes of Europe would be on Winchester, on the sealing of the alliance which would ensure for her son and Philip's the greater part of the West. They would be proclaimed "Philip and Mary, by the grace of God King and Queen of England, France, Naples, Jerusalem and Ireland, Defenders of the Faith, Princes of Spain and Sicily, Archdukes of Austria, Dukes of Milan, Burgundy and Brabant, Counts of Hapsburg, Flanders and Tyrol." But to her, overwhelmingly now, it was a man and a maid. She hoped desperately that he would like her and not find her too old.

She had done all she could, by public tokens, to reassure him. The outward show, which the country was discussing, would at least tell him her feelings. He could not know how pertinaciously she had fought her Councilors for the right to have him crowned, even though, with her mind, she had realized from the beginning that this could not be. But he might at least guess it when, before he had taken a step on English soil, he was invested with the Garter.

What she could neither mitigate nor control was the English weather. It was one of the worst Julys on record. As Philip was rowed from his ship to the quayside at Southhampton in the State Barge, manned by twenty men in the Tudor livery of green and silver, it began to rain. And it continued to rain for the next four days "without ceasing so much as an hour." In the rain, the Earl of Arundel, as Philip's foot touched the quay, bent to buckle the Garter and to invest him with the collar and mantle of the Order. In the rain, Philip accepted from the Master of the Horse, Mary's gift of a magnificent white genet, so

56

richly caparisoned in crimson and gold that, he remarked, "if his clothes were not fine enough for one about to marry so great a Queen, the bardings of the horse might do instead." Mounting it, he rode to the Church of the Holy Rood to give thanks for his safe arrival and then retired, thankfully, to the apartments that had been prepared for him to change his clothes and discard the necessity for charm. He noted, acidly, that the English in their desire for magnificence had overstepped the boundaries of tact. His room had been hung with the best royal arras the Crown possessed, but, either by accident or design, the Lord Chamberlain had omitted to notice that, in the embroidery, Henry VIII was described as "Defender of the Faith and Head of the Church."

On Monday, July 23, Mary made her public entry into Winchester in a furious storm of wind and rain and immediately sent off a courier to Philip to suggest that he remain in Southampton until the weather cleared a little. But Philip had already set out, wearing a thick red cloak over his black and white satin. Attended by his own extensive suite and accompanied by an English escort of two hundred and fifty superbly mounted knights under the Earl of Pembroke and a hundred archers, with their bows ready, dressed in the Spanish colors of crimson and gold, the stately procession was two miles out of Southampton before the courier arrived. Philip, who misunderstood the message and thought that Mary was warning him of a sudden insurrection against the marriage, summoned his Councilors for a roadside colloquy, which was abandoned only when an English nobleman, sensing cross-purposes, interrupted it and said in French: "Sire, our Queen lovingly greets Your Highness and has merely sent to say that she hopes you will not commence your journey to Winchester in such dreadful weather."

Philip, comprehending, gallantly decided to continue the journey and by the time that he had reached St. Cross, on the outskirts of Winchester, was, despite his thick cloak, soaked to the skin. He stopped there long enough to change into another suit of purple velvet richly embroidered with gold and to wrap himself in an even thicker, but dry, felt cloak and at last, just before seven in the evening, arrived at the city gate, to be met by the Mayor and Aldermen with the keys of the city and to be greeted with a great volley of artillery which told Mary, in the Bishop's Palace of Wolvesey, that the hour of meeting had come at last.

It was not till ten o'clock that night that he came to her. Since nine she had walked restlessly in the Long Gallery at Wolvesey, making no attempt to hide her impatience from her ladies, who shared it. At intervals, messengers sent out into the town brought news of his doings. He was at the Cathedral where Gardiner was singing a solemn Te Deum. The crush of people, in their thousands thronging to catch a glimpse of him, was so great that many had fainted and more were nearly suffocated . . . He had returned to the lodgings prepared for him at the Deanery and was supping quietly with Roy Gomez, his friend and Chamberlain, and a few other gentlemen . . .

Mary Browne, reading Mary's thoughts as this information was given her, said: "But the poor man must be starved. He has had no time to eat since he left Southampton. And in this weather!"

At last news was brought that the Prince was on his way, picking his way by torchlight through the sodden gardens. Fortunately the rain had ceased, though the trees

58

were still dripping ... Mary Browne quickly straightened
the Queen's head-dress of black and gold and smoothed
her gown; and when Philip entered by the Privy Stair,
his first impression of his bride was of a still, self-possessed
little woman, whose black and silver dress made her one
with the shadows and the sconces. In the candlelight, her
face was charming, and looked younger than he had expected.

She came toward him gravely, her galaxy of jewels
rainbowed in the light, and, with careful Spanish etiquette, kissed her own hand before she gave it to him. He
took it, but did not kiss it. Instead, "English fashion," he
kissed her on the mouth. Her pleasure at this was, however, lessened by the circumstance that he then greeted
each of her ladies in the same manner. That ritual ended,
they withdrew together into the further part of the Gallery, beyond the earshot of their attendants, and throughout the formal conversation—the weather, his journey,
their mutual gifts, the suitability of his lodgings, the arrangements for the wedding—she strove to assess the man
behind the mask.

Every time he looked away from her, she peered at him
with screwed-up eyes to see him the better. He was, she
decided, personable enough, though less handsome than
his portraits. His cane-colored complexion was not suited
to his fair hair and beard. His blue eyes were spoilt by the
heavy lids. She liked his erect carriage which gave the impression of more inches than he possessed, but she wished
he had been taller. To his real thoughts and feelings, she
had no clue; nor, fortunately, could she guess that he was
hoping his father would allow him to cross to Flanders
to join him in camp against the French as soon as the marriage was consummated. He had given orders to his fleet,

which was by now at Portsmouth, that nothing was to be disembarked until further orders.

Aloud, with his most charming smile, he said in Spanish: "Tell me, Mary, how to say 'Good night to you all' in English!'

She told him, laughing at him a little but secretly amazed at the quickness with which he picked it up. And when, ten minutes later he took his leave of her and said it to the English attendants, she joined them in praise of his accent . . .

"Well?" asked Mary Browne, after he had left.

"Well enough," said the Queen. "He has something of his father in him."

Next afternoon he visited her again, wearing the suit of gold-threaded brocade with pearl and diamond buttons which in the morning she had sent him as a gift. She welcomed him with all her musicians playing in the Great Hall of the Castle, beneath King Arthur's Round Table which had been newly painted in the Tudor green and white.

And in the evening he came once more bearing his father's final present about which he had been enjoined to keep silent till the very eve of the marriage. So that Mary the Queen should wed not a Prince but a King, Charles had relinquished his Kingdom of Naples to his son. Prince Philip was now King Philip and, as a King, would wed a Queen. It was a diplomatic masterstroke designed to please the English people, but Mary construed it, even if Philip did not, as Charles's private gesture of gratitude and remembrance.

St. James's Day dawned clear of rain, with the early morning mist giving promise of a perfect day. By half-past ten, Mary was ready in her wedding dress made in the new French style. Over the close-robe of white satin and silver, she wore a robe of rich brocade on a gold ground, with a long train bordered with pearls and diamonds of great size. The long sleeves were turned up with clusters of gold, also set with jewels, and her coif had on it two rows of large diamonds. Just before eleven she walked over in state to the Cathedral and in the choir she met Philip, dressed also in white, with a collar of beaten gold, diamond-studded. Together they proceeded to the chairs of state prepared for them, before the high altar.

Gardiner, who was to officiate, had already entered in such ecclesiastical state as only the old among the spectators could remember and which Winchester itself had not seen for centuries. He was accompanied by five other bishops—London, Durham, Chichester, Lincoln and Ely.

In the four-hour-long ceremony, there was only one moment of hesitation. The question "who was to give her?" had not been provided for. It took them all, as Gardiner asked it, unawares. Who, indeed, had that right other than Gardiner himself who, as Lord Chancillor, was keeper of her conscience? There was a pause and a rustle of whispers before the old Marquis of Winchester, who had been at her christening and who had proclaimed her Queen, stepped forward, with the Earls of Derby, Bedford and Pembroke, and gave her to Philip in the name of the whole realm of England.

Mary herself seemed unperturbed by the exigencies of ceremonial. She was, some thought, like a woman in a dream. Others, more observant, realized her recollection and noticed that, for an hour, she did not take her eyes from the Blessed Sacrament.

After the wedding, there was the banquet in the Great Hall of the Castle. King, Queen and Lord Chancellor ate

61

at the high table from gold plates and dishes under a canopy of crimson and gold. Musicians played, largesse was distributed, congratulatory odes were recited, speeches were made. There was dancing, led by the bride and bridegroom, in the German fashion. At last, in the glimmering dusk, they left the company to their revels and retired with Gardiner, who solemnly blessed the bridal bed before he left them to each other . . .

Philip, calling up in his memory the beauty of his first, dead wife and the bodies of women with whom, in debauches, he had sought to forget her, found suddenly in the darkness his fantasies dispelled by the actuality that Mary was, indeed, Henry's daughter.

# SEVEN

# Through
# Spanish
# Eyes

*A letter from a Gentleman
who accompanied
Prince Philip to England
written to a friend
in Spain*

Y OU WILL have heard that at Winchester
His Highness met the Queen, who had been waiting for
him there two weeks, and also that the wedding ceremonies were a fine sight, for there were six bishops in their
pontificals, with croziers and mitres. I have never seen so
many at any wedding.

Their Majesties are the happiest couple in the world and

63

more in love than words can say. His Highness never leaves her and when we are on the road he is always by her side, helping her to mount and dismount. They sometimes dine together in public and go to Mass together on Holy Days. The Queen, however, is not at all beautiful: small and rather flabby than fat, she is of white complexion and fair and has no eyebrows. She is a perfect saint and dresses badly.

All the women here wear petticoats of coloured cloth, without admixture of silk, and above come coloured robes of damask, satin or velvet, very badly cut. Their shoes are sometimes of velvet, but more often of leather, and they wear black stockings and show their legs up to the knee when walking. As their skirts are not long, they are passably immodest when walking and even when seated. They are neither beautiful nor graceful when dancing, and their dances only consist in strutting or trotting about. Not a single Spanish gentleman has fallen in love with any one of them nor takes any interest in them and their feelings for us are the same. They are not the sort of women for whom Spaniards feel inclined to take much trouble or to spend their money, which is an excellent thing for the Spaniards.

There are no distractions here except eating and drinking—the only amusement they understand. The Queen spends over 300,000 ducats a year on her table, for all thirteen Councillors eat in the Palace, as well as the household officers, the Master of the Horse, the Master of the Household (the Queen's as well as our own, for we also have English officers) and the wives of all these gentlemen into the bargain. The Queen's ladies also eat by themselves in the Palace, as well as all the councillors, governors and household officials. And then there are the two hundred

ENGRAVED FROM THE HOLBEIN ORIGINAL

"Little Edward, the stepbrother, was delicate;
Edward VI's reign was brief."

"So little Edward died, and Mary had to fight for her crown. . . ."

men of the guard. So all these ladies and gentlemen have their private quarters in the Palace and each gentleman has his cook in the Queen's kitchens, which cook looks only after his master.

There are usually eighteen kitchens in full blast and they seem veritable hells, such is the stir and bustle in them. The palaces here are enormous, for the smallest of the four we have seen is certainly much bigger and has more and larger apartments than the Alcazar of Madrid, but the throng of people is such that they are full to bursting. The usual daily consumption is eighty to a hundred sheep—and the sheep are very big and fat—a dozen fat oxen, a dozen and a half calves, without mentioning poultry, game, deer, boars and great numbers of rabbits.

There is plenty of beer here, and they drink more than would fill the Valladolid River. In the summer the ladies and some gentlemen put sugar in their wine, with the result that there are great goings-on in the Palace!

The English hate us Spaniards worse than they hate the Devil and treat us accordingly. Our lords have great trouble in finding lodgings. They rob us in town and on the road. There are an incredible number of robbers here; they go about in bands of twenty and neither justice nor fear of God avail to hold them back. No one ventures to stray two miles but they rob him, and a company of Englishmen have recently beaten and robbed over fifty Spaniards. The best of it is that the Councilors know all about it and do not say a word.

The King and Queen have no more authority in the realm than if they were vassals, for the Councilors govern and are the lords of the kingdom and even of the King and Queen. Some of these gentlemen are self-made, enriched by the rents torn from the Church which has been utterly overthrown; others were born to their estate and they are much more obeyed and looked up to than the King and Queen.

Mass is rarely celebrated and meagrely attended by a few who seem to hear it unwillingly; though wherever the Queen is, the Christian religion is kept up in all its dignity, for she is most holy and God-fearing. We went to London last Saturday (which we ought not to have done seeing the way we are treated there: even in the inns we are ill-treated and robbed) and saw it would have been well if His Highness had not brought the friars with him. The English are so bad and fear God so little that they handle the friars shamefully and the poor men do not dare leave their quarters. The Londoners tried to tear the cloaks from the backs of Don Pedro de Cordova and his nephew, Don Antonio, because, as Commendadores of our Military Orders, they had crosses on them. They jeered at them and asked what they meant by wearing crosses. Everything else goes to the same tune.

They say we shall not stay in London more than ten days and in October we shall go to another pleasure-house about four miles hence called Hampton Court, one of the finest and most commodious in the land. All the Queen's houses are well furnished with tapestries and most of the tapestries are adorned with sacred subjects, for they come from churches and monasteries which were destroyed in order to seize their revenues; and so the monks and nuns perished. It is said that two hundred monks and nuns were killed because they obeyed the Pope; and although that is a thing of the past, property from the churches and monasteries found its way into the exchequer to the amount of double the former royal revenues.

From the way things are going here, these godless folk

66

do not seem to be at all firm in matters of faith and will not make their submission to the Pope, but die stiff-necked heretics. Queen Mary—blessings on her—is beginning to set matters right, however, and a month before we arrived here she created a bishop because he had always been a good Christian.

The man who wrote *Amadis* and other books of chivalry, with all the flowery meads, pleasure-houses and enchantments, must first have visited England and seen the strange customs of the country. For who, in any other land, ever saw women riding forth alone as they do here, where many of them manage their horses with consummate skill and are as firm in the saddle as any man? I can assure you that there are more sights to be seen here than are described in any book of chivalry: country-houses, river-banks, woods, forests, delicious meadows, strong and beautiful castles and everywhere fresh springs; for all these things abound here and make the country well worth a visit and most delightful, especially in summer-time.

I could give you many more details of life here, but to avoid tiring you I will only say that we would rather be back in Spain than see England or the sea and we are all desiring to be off with such longing that we think even of Flanders as Paradise.

So now you may reflect on the way things are going in this realm. The match will have been a fine business if the Queen does not have a child; and I am sure she will not . . .

# EIGHT

# Elizabeth at Woodstock

A<small>T</small> W<small>OODSTOCK</small>, Sir Henry Bedingfield was finding his duties as Elizabeth's guardian little to his liking. It was an assignment that would have taxed the ablest diplomat and, as he was the first to admit, his "Norfolk understanding" was "not very nimble." He made no attempt to hide the fact that he would have considered his discharge "the joyfullest tidings that ever came to me, as Our Lord Almighty knoweth, from Whom no secrets are hid." But his loyalty to the Queen kept him at his post, ceaselessly alert.

He did not mind particularly when Elizabeth teased him by dragging him after her on a torrid afternoon from garden to garden, through various fields and finally to the orchard in search of a shady place to sit. That was natural enough. What worried him was that she misunderstood the nature of his responsibility. He was there to prevent her possible assassination and, in spite of the sixty men on guard by day and forty by night, it was impossible, without her co-operation, to be certain that she was safe. He was by no means satisfied that the fire which broke out under the floorboards of her bedchamber four days after she arrived was merely an unfortunate accident; and, during one of his short, enforced absences, a party of twenty-five disguised ruffians attempting to gain access to her on the plea of private and important business had been foiled only because of the acumen of his brother—the one man he dared to leave as deputy-castellan.

Yet Elizabeth insisted on addressing him as "My gaoler!" and when he knelt—he was always scrupulous to kneel when he spoke to her—to say: "I beseech Your Highness not to give me that harsh name, for I am one of your officers appointed to serve you and guard you from the dangers by which you are beset," she merely laughed.

It was, of course, true that he also had, as far as he could, to guard against the other and opposite danger of her continuing participation in plots against the Queen; but here, as he realized, adequate precautions were almost impossible. Greater men than he would have to concern themselves with that. All he could do was to point out to the Council that there were constant meetings at the Bull at Woodstock between Elizabeth's servants and some suspicious political characters and that that hostelry was "a marvellously colourable place to practice in."

Elizabeth was, in fact, in this way able to keep contact with her friends in the country and even to send messages and money to the imprisoned Archbishop of Canterbury, Thomas Cranmer, who a few miles away at Oxford was still contriving to make himself, by means of permitted theological discussions, a center of Protestant disaffection. She realized, however, that it was only by direct contact with the Queen that she could regain the full liberty so necessary to her and, hoping that Mary might be in a melting mood on the eve of her wedding, asked permission to write to her. Bedingfield delivered the message and received the reply that "the Lady Elizabeth's Grace may write to Her Highness according to her desire."

Elizabeth's missive was almost a repetition, though more carefully and elegantly phrased, of her desparing appeal when she was ordered to the Tower. Once more she denied any correspondence with "that traitor Wyatt." Once more she denied any collusion with the French Ambassador. With a flourish she asserted: "May God confound me if I did!"

It was unfortunate that a copy of this letter, too, found its way into de Noailles's hands and was in due course intercepted by the Council. Consequently, when Elizabeth asked Bedingfield whether there had been any reply to her letter, he had to say: "I have an answer to declare whenever Your Grace shall be pleased to hear it" in a tone which warned her that the news was not palatable.

"Let it be at once," she said; but, no sooner had he gone to fetch the document, than she sent a servant after him to tell him to wait till she had dined.

Even dinner did not fortify her sufficiently to receive the message with equanimity and after he had read it, kneeling, she asked him to read it again while she recovered her selfcontrol and thought of an answer.

Mary had addressed the letter to Bedingfield: "We were at the beginning most sorry to have any cause of suspicion; but when it appeared unto us that the copies of her private letters to us were found in the packets of the French Ambassador and that divers of the most notable traitors made their chief account upon her, we can hardly be brought to think that they would have pre-

sumed to do so unless they had more certain knowledge
of her favour towards their unnatural conspiracy than she
has as yet confessed. Therefore, though we have on our
part (considering what has been brought to our knowledge against her) used more clemency toward her than
had been customary in such matters, yet her fair words
cannot so deceive us that we do not well understand how
these things have been wrought. The Queen desires you
not to let her be any more molested by such dishonest and
colourable letters."

When she had heard it the second time, Elizabeth answered: "I note especially to my great discomfort, though
I shall nevertheless obey, that the Queen's Majesty is not
pleased that I should 'molest' her Highness with any more
of my 'colourable letters.' Although she terms them colourable yet I must say for myself that what I wrote was
plain truth, as I desire to be saved before God Almighty.
But let it pass!" She then asked Bedingfield to convey her
answer on the royal message to the Council and communi-
cate their reply to her. Sir Henry excused himself and
withdrew.

Next day, walking in the Privy Garden, she returned
to the attack.

"Sir Henry."

"Your Grace."

"Yesterday you absolutely refused to write on my behalf to the Council."

"Madame, it was neither my place to do so nor would
it have served any purpose. Her Majesty is not likely so
soon to change her mind."

"Unless you change *your* mind," retorted Elizabeth,
"I shall be in a worse case than the worst prisoner in New-
gate. At least they are not prevented having their cause

considered, while I must continue in this life without worldly hope, trusting wholly to the truth of my cause before God, arming myself against whatever may happen to remain the Queen's true subject, as I have done during my life."

Before Bedingfield could think of a reply to the prepared periods, she darted away with: "It's going to rain, so I will go back to the house."

If he would not write to the Council about the Queen's letter, he should at least be made, she determined, to write about her own health. A refusal on that score would be impossible. There was no doubt that her face was swollen and that she constantly felt ill. She had been complaining about it for some time. Her arms, too, were swelling. Mary must send her one of the family doctors.

When five pens, two sheets of paper and a standish were brought, she wrote the letter, complained of a pain in her head and asked Sir Henry to copy out to her dictation what she had written. He asked to be excused because of his bad writing.

"I never write to the Lords of the Council except by a secretary," said Elizabeth haughtily, "and seeing that at this time I am not allowed to have one, you must do it."

"I pray Your Grace to pardon me," said Bedingfield, "but I am unable."

This time she was adamant. He wrote the letter.

The answer was as unsatisfactory as ever. It was that Dr. Hughes was too ill to come and that neither Dr. Owen nor Dr. Wendy could at the moment be spared from Court. Dr. Owen, however, recommended two honest and learned physicians at Oxford, of great skill, either or both of whom she might send for.

73

"I will make arrangements at once, Your Grace, to have them brought over."

"You can spare your pains, Sir Henry," said Elizabeth. "I shall not see them. I have no mind to make any stranger privy to the state of my body, but commit it to God."

The tedium of the summer, accentuated by the reports that reached her of the gaieties of the Court, came at last to an end, leaving her resentment against her sister too profound ever to be eradicated. Her decision that it would be politic for her to conform to Catholicism only served to increase it and just before her first Mass she was careful to leave evidence of her devotion to the Protestant "religion of the Bible" by inscribing on the flyleaf of a copy of St. Paul's Epistles: "August—I walked many times into the pleasant fields of the Holy Scriptures, where I pluck up the goodlisome herbs of sentences by pruning, eat them by reading, chew them by musing and lay them up at length in the high seat of memory by gathering them together; that so, having tasted their sweetness, I may the less perceive the bitterness of this miserable life."

She continued to complain of her health and with the coming of autumn she was sufficiently indisposed for Mary to send both Dr. Owen and Dr. Wendy to Woodstock, accompanied by a surgeon to bleed her if necessary. The treatment proved effective but what aided her recovery even more was the opportunity it gave her to persuade them to intercede for her with her sister. Impressed by her pathos and innocence, the old men promised to do their best and inspired her with new hope. All would be well at last, she felt, now that the approach to the Queen came from within what was, after all, the family circle.

Neither she nor they were in a position to know that

Renard, who was in constant touch with Philip and Mary, thought it worth while to report the following week in his letter to the Emperor Charles: "A few days ago Elizabeth sent for the Queen's physicians, who bled her to stop a running cold in the head from which she was suffering. It is suspected here that the French are continuing their intrigues with her and that some of her relatives are in touch with the French Ambassador."

# NINE

# Spanish
# Comment

*A further letter from a Gentleman
who accompanied
Prince Philip to England
written to a friend
in Salamanca*

I<small>N MY</small> letter from Richmond I gave you an account of everything that had happened since my landing and I am now writing again in obedience to your wishes and shall be exceedingly happy to do so as often as you wish. Indeed, were you not to ask me I should feel injured.

The news I now have to give you are that most of the Spaniards who came here with His Majesty have been indisposed and some of them really ill, apparently because

77

of the change of climate. Such are the misfortunes that await us in this country. The country itself is, it is true, a good one, but we are surrounded by the worst people that ever lived, at any rate in a Christian land. The English hate us Spaniards, which comes out in violent quarrels between them and us, and not a day passes without some knife-work in the Palace between the two nations. There have already been some deaths and in the last week of September three Englishmen and a Spaniard were hanged on account of a brawl.

There is certainly much to be seen in this country, especially in the great and populous cities like London where we now are—a capital full of magnificent things, grand buildings and noteworthy achievements of industry. But there are many thieves here, who live on the fruits of their thefts. We have been warned to go home before it gets dark and stay within doors; for otherwise we have to be very careful if we do not wish to lose our cloaks and our lives. That is the sort of life we lead here, though the officers of justice severely punish as many robbers as they can catch.

Think of it, only the other day they hanged an Englishman here for stealing fourteen pence, which by Castilian reckoning amounts to less than two and a half *reales*, for the penny they use here is worth about six of ours. And in spite of such severity there are so many thieves that as I have said no one must walk the streets after night-fall. Another great drawback here is the dearness of everything, for all prices have risen enormously of late years, especially those of food. So the gentlemen who came with His Highness and thought that ten, for instance, would be enough, find that they need a hundred or more.

We Spaniards move among the English as if they were

animals, trying not to notice them and they do the same to us. They refuse to crown our Prince, though he is their King, for they do not recognise him as such, but merely as one who has come to act as governor of the realm and to get the Queen with child. When she has had children of him, they say, he may go home to Spain. Would to God it might happen at once, for it would be a good thing for him and I believe he would be very glad! All of us would certainly be delighted to get away from these barbarous folk.

The Queen is said to be with child, though we know nothing more than what is being said in the Palace. The King has paid her debts to the tune of over 250,000 ducats and has also distributed over 30,000 ducats worth of pensions among the Council and great lords to keep them contented. So you see what profit Spain is going to realise from this marriage! And even after all this, the English will have none of us. My own conviction is that, were it not that Our Lord is watching over us in answer to the ceaseless prayers and processions which, so your letter tells me, are being held in Spain, we should all be dead by now; for these barbarous English heretics are void of soul or conscience, fear neither God nor His Saints and refuse obedience to the Pope who, they say, is a man like themselves and has no right to order them to do this or that; so the only Pope they recognise is their King, or as at present their Queen, who may command them to do or not anything she pleases.

A week ago Parliament opened after the accustomed Mass of the Holy Ghost in the church of Westminster, at which the King and Queen assisted, clothed as follows: a great tunic down to the feet and over it a mantle of crimson velvet with a very long train and lined with ermine thickly dotted with black spots, a large hood of the same covering the shoulders. On their heads they wore only caps and the tippet, their Majesties' usual adornment, but two lords carried before them two bonnets of crimson velvet also lined with spotted ermine. Two other lords carried before them two great swords as signs of power, but many people were of the opinion that one of these swords would have been enough, as husband and wife are one and the same thing. Then there were four mace-bearers with the arms of England, four pursuivants with damask coats after a different pattern from those worn by the heralds, but I do not know exactly what the office of these pursuivants may be. In front of the last named came a great company of trumpeters, preceded in their turn by thirteen bishops and a large number of lords.

The whole company marched in procession to church, the King on horseback and the Queen in a sort of litter, open so as quite to expose her to the public view. The crush of people in palace and church was such that it was almost impossible to move. I believe there must have been 20,000 persons present. The people showed a wonderful enthusiasm for their Majesties and I saw many signs of love and good will that I could hardly believe, except that the English are always in a good temper if they have a spectacle to watch. There were such exclamations as: "O, how handsome the King is!" "O, how kind and gentle he looks!" "O, what a good husband he is! How lovingly he treats the Queen!" After Mass, when their Majesties were on their way from the choir of the church to the Parliament house, an old woman cried out: "An evil death to the traitors who said that our King was mis-shapen! Look at him! He is as fair as an angel! And I hear that he is good, holy and pious! God save him and bless us!"

At Mass the Bishop of Lincoln preached a sermon in English, though at the end he summed it up in Latin so that the King might understand it, taking as his text the words of Jeremiah: *My thoughts are thoughts of peace.* He said that those who separated from the Primitive Church, which was the Roman Apostolic Church in succession from St. Peter, did not harbour thoughts of peace, any more than did the introducers of new religions and new dogmas, or the seditious, or those who were disobedient to the King, the Queen or their magistrates. Now was the time to hand back the keys to the keeper of keys, the Pope and to establish firmly the true Catholic religion.

To this end, to reconcile the country to the Holy See and absolve it from the blasphemies that have been committed, Cardinal Pole, otherwise known as His Eminence of England, who has been kept waiting a long time in Flanders, is now coming hither. Some of the foremost members of the Council and the Master of the Horse have gone to conduct him hither and he is expected daily. Great advantages to religious and secular affairs are looked for from his presence, for he is highly thought of as a Christian and a good man. The holders of Church property have not been asked to make any sacrifices but are going to be left undisturbed. I believe this is the main reason why they have given their consent to his admission, though some say that, if the lands are not given back, it will be treason to Our Lord and that the reign even of so good and religious a Queen will come to disaster on account of it.

It is believed that the King will certainly go to Flanders after Christmas to visit his father, the Emperor, and we

Spaniards hope that we shall be able to accompany him and leave this country for ever. The Cardinal's coming may make such a thing easier. Meanwhile it is impossible to be blind to certain dangers. One of the great lords, the Earl of Derby, found a letter when walking, so adroitly thrown down in front of him that he could not help picking it up. The gist of it was that, if he attended Parliament, he would lose his head and to advise him to beware of making any concessions to the Spaniards, whose object was to seize the kingdom by force, and to remember that the Queen had usurped a crown to which she had no right. This has so greatly irritated Parliament that measures are being taken for the punishment of slanderers, but, as you will have understood from my account of these people, to make a law is not the same as enforcing it or finding the culprits . . .

POSTSCRIPT: I have heard that the Cardinal has landed at Dover and is now at Canterbury. He is to proceed from Gravesend by water and the King will receive him at the riverside, for the Thames flows past the royal house of Westminster.

# The Cardinal Legate

$M$ARY AND PHILIP were still at dinner when news came that the Cardinal's barge was at the water-gate. The tide had proved so favorable that he was before his expected time. Philip rose at once and hurried to welcome him. Mary, with her chief lady-in-wating, Catherine Pole, the Cardinal's niece, went more slowly to await him at the top of the stairs.

This was the moment for which she had prayed and fought. Pole brought the pardon for England's apostasy. In ending his own long exile, he ended, too, his country's exile from the Faith. She was aware of the cheering of the people along the banks of the Thames as a murmur, far off, and, nearer, the excited shouts and conversation as in the courtyard the procession was forming behind the great silver crucifix which had been brought in from the prow of his barge. A sudden, spontaneous cheer told her that Philip was greeting the Legate. She made an act of thanksgiving. Then, unexpectedly and irrationally, the personal usurped all her mind. How would Reynald look? Would the years have changed him beyond recognition? And what would he think of her?

She had not seen him for nearly a quarter of a century, since that day, her sixteenth birthday, when he had ridden over to Ampthill to take farewell of his mother, her governess, and also—so she had liked to think—of her. He was nearly thirty-two (his birthday was a fortnight after hers) and she saw him always in her mind as he had been then, with a new sadness in his eyes and the mouth, not hidden by his short, fair beard, set grimly. Tall, elegant, graceful as a leopard, looking every inch the Plantagenet prince he was, he seemed the embodiment of impersonal courtesy, remote even in crisis. He had just refused the Archbishopric of York, her father's bribe to him for complaisance in the matter of divorcing her mother, and his sudden surge of uncontrollable anger with the King had meant an end of their friendship. And now that he was going into his self-imposed exile, Mary had realized that another chapter of her youth was ended. He would not come back. She would not be his wife, after all.

If the disappointment had not had the edge of Charles's rejection of her, it was more pervasive, for the figure of Reynald had filled the interim of those seven years of girlhood after the Emperor's defection. The fact that he was a man, the same age as Charles, was to her no drawback, for that was how she had come to imagine her husband. And if she saw Pole seldom, because of his studies in Italy, it was, even so, oftener than she had seen Charles. Moreover, the marriage to Pole had been planned even

84

before her father's diplomatic needs dictated the choice of the Emperor. When she was in her cradle, her mother and Pole's had planned it. And it held a deeper than diplomatic import. It was an atonement.

When her grandfather, Ferdinand of Aragon, had permitted her mother's marriage to the Prince of Wales, he had made one terrible condition with the Prince's father. Henry Tudor, the seventh King of that name, held the throne of England by right of conquest and a doubtful descent. The Plantagenets were conquered and deposed; most were dead. Yet one legitimate heir remained, Edward IV's eldest nephew, Edward, Earl of Warwick and Salisbury. From the age of ten, the victorious Henry Tudor had kept him in close confinement, deliberately deprived him of education and had him treated like a half-imbecile peasant. Yet as long as he lived, the rightful Plantagenet King of England, there was danger to the new line; and the cynical realist, Ferdinand, had no intention of allowing his daughter, Catherine, to marry into a *parvenu* dynasty without that danger, at least, being disposed of. Warwick must die before Catherine of Aragon's marriage to the Prince of Wales took place.

There had been no difficulty. Henry VII had welcomed the excuse and the judicial murder was speedily arranged. The twenty-one-year-old Edward was executed on the false charge of conspiring against the throne; while his sister, Margaret, to counter her lineage, was married off to an obscure knight, Sir Richard Pole.

Catherine of Aragon was from the first haunted by the fact that her marriage had been thus made in blood, and on her arrival in England, she sought out Margaret Pole, appointed her her first lady and made her her closest friend.

Later she had prevailed on her husband, Henry VIII, to restore something of Margaret's inheritance and to bestow on her the family title of Countess of Salisbury in her own right. Not only, in due time, did she appoint her governess to her own child Mary, but she ensured also that Margaret's son, Reginald, was educated at the Royal expense. Still this was not enough. Mary and Reginald must marry and, by their union, atone for the sin in which her own marriage was rooted.

When Mary was, by her father's orders, separated from her mother and sent to hold a lonely court as Princess of Wales at Ludlow, she found in her governess a second mother indeed. It seemed that Reginald, occasionally journeying to visit them from the monastery at Sheen, was an elder brother rather than a prospective bridegroom. Though he was in deacon's orders and a prebendary of Salisbury Cathedral he had no intention of becoming a priest. He would remain free to marry . . . That, perhaps, was his one, unspoken concession to the arrangement. He was charming to her, but even in her early teens, she had been quite aware that his attitude to her was that of a brother rather than a lover. It was in her talks with his mother that she had thought in other terms, as she watched while the Countess, in her exquisite embroidery, made a child's vest in which the Arms of England were surrounded by their entwined devices—the marigolds of Mary and the heart's-ease of Pole.

And now Reginald was home again, still, though Cardinal of England, only in deacon's orders, and she was married to Philip. Yet the past was still potent in the present. In this moment, as the sounds of his approach grew nearer and she realized its power, not, indeed over herself—how could she love anyone but Philip now she had tasted love?

—but over the cause to which she was dedicated. Had Reginald, after all, come too late?

Had she had her way, he would have been at her side sixteen months ago, at the very beginning of her reign. She would have made him Archbishop of Canterbury. He would have crowned her. But Charles had arranged otherwise. The Emperor had involved Pole in diplomatic business, intrigued at Rome to keep him from England, refused him, in the end, a safe-conduct through Europe or facilities to cross the Channel. He had extracted from her that strange oath that if she did not marry Philip, she would marry no one. She had, indeed, been the more willing to take that oath because Reynald had written to her urging her not to marry at all, but to take up the unheard-of burden of being the first Queen Regnant of England, alone and unwed, trusting solely to God to sustain her.

Now, at last, as Pole came in sight, a tall, thin old man in the vivid scarlet of his Cardinal's robes, she realized, in a flash, the full force of the implications to which she had been blind. The oath had been directed against him. The delays had been invented to keep him from her. At last she saw clearly what all Europe had been watching with amusement—how the Emperor had prevented Pole going to England before its Queen was safely married to his son for fear that, otherwise, she would have married Pole. Marveling at her obtuseness, she saw, too, in that instant, something of the calamity of the decision. With Reginald as King-Consort instead of Philip—a loved Plantagenet instead of a hated Spaniard—the country would have been unshakably hers. There would have been no insurrections; French intrigues would have been powerless; Elizabeth would have been no danger to the Throne. Already the Faith would have been re-established without fear of overthrow. That was the price she had unwittingly paid for Philip. Had she, in her happiness with him, been led into a betrayal of what most she loved?

The momentary panic passed. It was the future, after all, which would decide. And the future was the son she would bear to Philip, the son who, joining England, Spain and the Empire, would be the greatest Catholic king in Europe. She had no doubt that it would be a boy . . .

They were mounting the steps now, Philip arm-in-arm with the Cardinal, unobtrusively helping him. By contrast with her husband's vivid youth, Mary thought, Reynald looked even older than he was. His shoulders were bowed; his long beard was graying; his face, pale and lined, was emaciated with fasting; his eyes held more sadness even than she remembered in them. Then, looking up at her, he smiled and, on a sudden, was himself again, recognizable beyond doubt. She made a formal obeisance; then, impulsively, as he bowed to her, kissed him on both cheeks.

"Reynald, how good that you are here. I am happier today than when I took the throne."

Before he could answer, Philip interrupted saying, in Latin: "Let up put the Queen between us." He ranged himself on her left, leaving Pole the place of honor. So, to the sound of the silver trumpets, the three passed through the King's Hall.

Mary was seized by an urgent desire to explain to him why his recall had been so long delayed. She found herself inventing excuses for Charles and taking the responsibility on herself. The situation in England was so difficult . . . It was essential not to move too fast in undoing the heresy to which many had grown accustomed . . . The restoration of Church property affected the outlook even

88

of good Catholics . . . Philip, amused, gazed in front of him, his eyes masked in impassivity, while Pole, charming, answered her volubility with: "Let us not disturb the past when the present has been brought to such a happy issue. You are here, Mary, supported by the two greatest powers on earth—the Emperor, represented by the King, your husband, and the Pope represented by me."

"All the past, Reynald?"

She had to ask it now. He understood that and answered with simple directness: "Only one question. Did my mother suffer greatly? I heard they had a bungling executioner."

The vision of blood, the new blood added to the old that had haunted all their lives, was dizzying. She felt the need to exorcise it by calling it up in formal, unnecessary words: "When my father killed your mother——" But she could not go on. The actual image of her beloved governess, as the Protestant Bishop Latimer had described to her with cruel relish, hacked to death at the age of seventy on Tower Green by a youth horror-crazed by his own incompetence, still sickened her. At least she could save Reynald that. A lie was permissible. "No," she said, "it was a tale they put round, hoping it would reach you in Italy and increase your sorrow."

Pole accepted the comfort without believing it. "She was well," he asked, "when she saw you last?"

"Yes, but I think she knew she would have to die for the Faith and would not see you again. She asked me to give you her rosary. They took everything else from her. I have used it myself always, since."

"Both she and I would wish you to keep it, Mary, if you will."

89

Philip interrupted: "There is much justice to be done, my Lord Cardinal, on wicked men."

"Certainly," said Pole, "we must all see that my mother and the other martyrs did not give their blood in vain. We will make a Christian England for your son to rule."

That night, when Pole had returned to the apartments prepared for him in Lambeth Palace across the river, he was roused to receive a special message the Queen had sent to him. She wrote that she had now no doubt that she was pregnant. As he arrived she had felt the child stir in her womb. Would he arrange that a solemn *Te Deum* should be sung in all the churches in London?

# ELEVEN

# The Ambassadors Report

*Simon Renard to the Emperor Charles V*
London, November 30, 1554

. . . Cardinal Pole arrived here about two o'clock in the afternoon of Saturday last. Yesterday Parliament came to the unanimous decision that all laws and statutes contrary to the Pope's authority should be repealed, the Church's authority once more acknowledged and the Cardinal admitted as Legate to carry out his mission and play the part of a welcome mediator. Your Majesty too well understands how great was the joy felt by the King and all his Court for it to be necesary for me to describe it. Indeed, he had good reason to render thanks to God that such fruit, fertile in increase of authority for him, should already have come of the match, encouraging us to hope that God means to incline the enemy's heart to desire lasting peace . . .

## The Ambassadors Report

### Don Pedro de Cordova to the King of the Romans
London, December 19, 1554

. . . The Queen has shown herself to be the thorough Christian she is, the King has not made things more difficult and Our Lord has not forgotten the good lady, for she is certainly with child and is expected to be confined in April. These news are so good that there is no time to write about anything else. The royal couple are well, and are loved and obeyed by their subjects. In the chapel and all the London churches a *Te Deum* was sung for the Queen's pregnancy. May God deliver her and give her the son these realms so sorely need . . .

### Memorandum from Simon Renard to King Philip
December 1554

. . . Report has it that Your Majesty is shortly to leave England. I hear that the Queen has been informed that Your Majesty means to depart for Flanders before her delivery, about which she is greatly distressed, fearing for her life and her child's if you go before she is confined . . .

### Giovanni Michiel to the Doge and Senate of Venice
London, March 19, 1555

. . . The Queen has sent for many friars of the Orders of St. Dominic and St. Francis who, to escape past persecutions, withdrew beyond the sea and lived in poverty in Flanders, in order to give them monasteries and means of subsistence; and they, showing themselves in public everywhere, are tolerably well received and kindly treated. Sixteen Benedictine monks have also reassumed the habit and returned to the Order spontaneously, although they were able to live, and had lived, out of it much at ease and liberty; notwithstanding which they have renounced all their temporal possessions and conveniences and press for readmission into one of their monasteries. The entire sixteen last week appeared in their habits before the Queen who, from joy, immediately on seeing them could not refrain from shedding tears.

On the other hand, Londoners do not desist from daily outrages against the Catholic religion, having not only again mutilated the statue of St. Thomas of Canterbury, which had been restored and put back in its place, but even robbed several churches of the tabernacles of the Blessed Sacrament. Nor, at least at this commencement, does the government think fit to act with such rigour as is becoming, hoping that, by address and leniency, Time, rather than severe punishment, may mitigate this their rage and fury . . .

### *The Same to the Same*
London, March 26, 1555

The Lords of the Council have lately had suspicion that certain inhabitants of Cambridge, more daring and licentious than the rest, not choosing to inconvenience themselves by living according to the present religion, had leagued together and secretly collected a large supply of arms for a rising when the moment should seem propitious, not merely to conspire against the loyalists and the Catholics (termed by them 'Papists') but, with numerous adherents they expected to have, march upon this city, hoping, with the assistance of the Londoners who share their opinions, not merely by slaughter and torture to expel all foreigners hence, but even to attack their Majesties and, under the pretext of religion, kindle such a flame and cause such a confusion as is in their power, to the detriment and perhaps utter ruin of the King and Queen, as the authors of this return to Catholicism.

In order to convince themselves and verify the suspicion and danger, the Lords of the Council immediately caused the arrest and removal to the Tower of many of the inhabitants of Cambridge, including one of the gentry of the place, Antony Bowes, a man utterly averse to religion; and other arrests are made daily in this town, the prisoners being strictly examined to ascertain the origin and basis of the plot and detect the conspirators.

An act of justice is expected, it appearing to everybody that the graciousness and clemency hitherto exercised by their Majesties in pardoning everybody, especially the Ipswich people who laid a similar plot last summer, merely give cause, through hope of pardon, for the daily perpetration of fresh excesses, instead of mitigating or eradicating the ill will of persons of this sort . . .

*Simon Renard to the Emperor Charles V*
London, March 27, 1555

. . . It has been ascertained that several gentlemen and others had proposed to publish broadsheets in several regions of this kingdom proclaiming that subjects will no longer allow the common land and pastures to be enclosed, but demand that they be open for the common people. Also, to proclaim the new religion, against the Acts of Parliament and the authority of the Pope. Also, to set the Lady Elizabeth free and to marry her to Courtenay. Also,

94

to publish that the Queen is not with child, but that there was a plan to pass off another child as her own. It should be remembered that religion is not yet firmly established and that the heretics are on the watch for every possible opportunity to revive error and compromise the good beginning that has been made. The kingdom is in uncertainty as to the succession to the Crown. Supposing the Queen is not with child and dies without issue, the heretics will espouse the cause of the Lady Elizabeth . . .

*Giovanni Michiel to the Doge and Senate of Venice*
London, April 1, 1555

. . . To comfort the Queen and give her heart and courage, three most beautiful infants were brought last week for Her Majesty to see, they having been born a few days previously at one birth, of a woman of low stature and advanced age, like the Queen and who, after delivery, found herself strong and out of all danger. The sight of this woman and her infants greatly rejoiced Her Majesty.

*Simon Renard to the Emperor Charles V*
London, April 4, 1555

. . . The officers of the law who have been investigating the criminal charges about which I have already written to Your Majesty have announced that the persons who had been arrested for conspiracy and sedition do not appear to have been as guilty as had been supposed. Thus the proceedings have cooled off, or as some say have been hushed up.

Some people think that the matter is made little of in order not to alarm the Queen, who is approaching her

confinement. The King and Queen are leaving today for
Hampton Court . . .

### Giovanni Michiel to the Doge and Senate of Venice
London, April 8, 1555

Edward Courtenay, Earl of Devonshire, has at length
obtained his complete release through the graciousness
and clemency of Their Majesties and is to go to Court
this day to kiss hands. It will soon be followed by that of
the Lady Elizabeth likewise. This act is the more agreeable to the whole kingdom as it was quite unexpected,
everybody supposing that it would not be thought of until after the Queen's delivery; but the prudence and judgment of these princes have made them choose to render
their clemency and liberality more manifest by demonstrating it precisely at this most critical moment and rely-
ing on popular opinion and, more especially, on the nobility of the personages.

A few days ago, forty miles from here in the county
of Essex, a slight insurrection occurred on account of religion. Lord Dacre having, by order of the government,
escorted certain heretics condemned to be burnt, so great
a concourse of persons assembled at this spectacle that it
was incredible. When about to be executed, they ve-
hemently exhorted the multitude to persevere in their
religion and endure, as they themselves were doing, any
persecution or any torment; which so moved the people
that the Governor was apprehensive of an attack on himself and his officials, very strong language having been
used against those who ordered the execution and passed
sentence on men of such piety and constancy whom they,
the people, considered the holiest of martyrs.

*The Same to the Same*

London, April 15, 1555

. . . Cardinal Pole's indisposition, which at first sight seemed not to be severe, increased so violently, a malignant fever having never left him for five consecutive days that not only his own attendants but the physicians themselves despaired of his life. But through the aid and grace of the Almighty, he is now out of danger, though so weak and exhausted that all who see him know well how he must have suffered.

Yesterday, Easter Day, a great outrage was committed in the parish church of St. Margaret, Westminster, for while the priest was standing at the altar with the ciborium in his hand, full of consecrated wafers, giving communion to the parishioners, he was suddenly assaulted by an Englishman, with a naked sword in his hand and in a violent rage who, after saying that by the idolatry he was committing he was deceiving the many souls there assembled, with other blasphemous language, gave him two such deep wounds, one on the hand and the other on the head, that he fell as if dead, causing such an uproar and tumult that it was wonderful.

Persons who did not know the cause and especially strangers, believed that the English had risen for the purpose of killing the Spaniards and all the other foreigners who dwell for the most part in that quarter. Everybody, more especially the Spaniards, were in great alarm. But, on hearing what had happened, quiet was restored and the malefactor seized . . .

97

# The Ambassadors Report

### Simon Renard to the Emperor Charles V
Twickenham, April 21, 1555

. . . It has been decided to bring Elizabeth here to Court in a few days, before the Queen's confinement takes place. The Queen has withdrawn and no one enters her apartments except the women who serve her and who have the same duties as the Court officials. This is an ancient custom in England whenever a Princess is about to be confined: to remain in retirement forty days before and forty days after. However, it is believed that she will be delivered before the ninth day of next month. She would have liked to go to Windsor, but as that place is far from London, it was thought preferable that she should stay at Hampton Court. Troops will be at hand in case they are needed . . .

### Giovanni Michiel to the Doge and Senate of Venice
London, April 29, 1555

By my letters of the 8th instant, I wrote it was hoped soon to witness the release of the Lady Elizabeth, so I now inform you that today or tomorrow, she will certainly be at Court with Their Majesties, whence, for very good reasons, she will not depart until after the Queen's delivery. It is supposed that, in the event of the Queen's death (from which may God preserve us) the King's safety and security would depend more on her than on any other person. With the favour of the great men here whom he has already gained by rewards, he might hope to succeed to the kingdom by making a second marriage with her. It is probable that she also might spontaneously incline that way, as she is well acquainted with his actions and character. Yet even should she, or the country, deny him this, yet by her presence here in his power he would at least expect to secure himself better against any rising or danger to himself and his followers. They would all, under her favour, be able to depart at leisure and in safety . . .

*Simon Renard to the Emperor Charles V*
Twickenham, May 6, 1555

. . . The Lady Elizabeth is here at Court. The King considers that it would be better to keep her here until after the Queen's confinement; and there may be something in this as the confinement is so near. However, the Queen's Council think that it would be safer to have her out of the country, either before or after.

*Giovanni Michiel to the Doge and Senate of Venice*
London, May 6, 1555

On Tuesday, the last day of April, at daybreak, a report circulated that the night before, half an hour after midnight, the Queen had been delivered of a male child with little pain and no danger. Owing to this news, as firmly believed and asserted by everyone, even by the magistrates and the royal officials, the people made public demonstrations of joy by shutting the shops, processions in the churches, ringing the bells. Public tables were spread with wine and viands for all comers; and, although it was day, there were bonfires in the streets. But in the afternoon, several persons having returned from Hampton Court with a truer account, the falsity was made manifest for not only had the delivery not taken place, but neither had any of the symptoms which precede delivery manifested

99

themselves. It is difficult to express how much this dispirited everybody.

The original source of this report is not yet known, but many people suppose it to have been done designedly rather than by accident.

The Lady Elizabeth came to Court very privately, accompanied by three or four of her women and as many male servants; but was neither met nor received by anyone. She was given the apartments which the Duke of Alva had recently used and lives there in retirement.

# TWELVE

# Meeting at Night

Elizabeth in the richly-furnished apartments kept for distinguished foreign visitors in the Water Gallery by the river at Hampton Court, was chiefly concerned about her Oratory. She insisted that it should be decorated with every token of piety she possessed, so that, should Mary decide to pay her a sudden visit, she would find her there, on her knees, and would entertain no doubt about the genuineness of her Catholicism. She was also careful always to carry the rosary of white coral beads on a gold chain which Mary had given her.

Sir William Cecil, on his last visit to her at Woodstock, had emphasized that it was impossible to be too ostentatious in such things. This Protestant politician, in his middle thirties, was now never seen without an enormous rosary hanging from his girdle. His public display of devotion bordered on the fantastic. He even helped to instruct the congregation at his local church in the mysteries of the Faith and at Easter was the first to go publicly to confession. She would not have been surprised if he had imitated Louis XI of France, whom he resembled in mind and body, by wearing little images of the saints round his hat. But when she had taxed him with extravagance, he had merely quoted sententiously: "Si fueris Romae, Romano vivito more" and added: "For us, Your Highness, it is the only way to be certain of living at all. And none of our *friends* will be deceived."

At the beginning, Elizabeth was inclined to wonder whether Mary was deceived either, but events had forced her to the conclusion that her sister was as simple as she seemed. As soon as she had told Mary of her desire to be a Catholic and blamed her Protestantism on the influence of her elderly lady-in-waiting, Lady Catherine Grey, everything became easy. In spite of the guards at Woodstock, in spite of Sir Henry Bedingfield's continuing conscientiousness, she had been able without difficulty to take her place at the center of the web of intrigue.

Her friends were not impeded in their visits. Sir William Cecil could come and advise her on the property he had always managed for her in her brother's time, discussing such business as rents and the sale of timber. The ebullient young Henry Carey, her first cousin, son of Anne Boleyn's sister, could entertain her with stories of his travels abroad. Other amusing visitors were occasionally introduced by her two long-standing attendants, Thomas Parry, her shrewd, worldy-wise cofferer, and Kate, her governess, who had married another of her cousins, John Ashley. There was nothing to prevent them at any time from walking together in the grounds of Woodstock, where none could overhear their discussion, as they gave direction to the outbreaks which kept the government in a state of exasperated tension.

Within a month of Mary's accession, Cecil had begun to create his now-effective revolutionary organization. From London a secret committee of twenty-six men whose power and wealth, like his own, were derived from the plunder of churches and monasteries, directed and financed the six hundred or so "students," bankers, writers and ministers who had emigrated immediately after Lady Jane Grey's attempt to dethrone Mary had failed. These were concentrated as self-contained English communities in five towns in Germany and Switzerland where they acted as centers of training and intrigue for dethroning and murdering Mary and making Elizabeth Queen in her place. From their main office in Emden, which was directed by Cecil's brother-in-law, scurrilous pamphlets and seditious propaganda were taken across the Channel by special "messengers" and disseminated in Kent and East Anglia. The London storehouse was Elizabeth's own palace of Somerset House where Thomas Parry, as her man of affairs, saw to it that no one suspected old lumber in the cellars.

Henry Carey, during his insouciant travels on the Continent, co-ordinated the communities on matters of high policy and on his return made reports to Cecil; and John Ashley, in conjugal letters to Kate, could deal with any topic which might arise unexpectedly. Those Protestant bankers who had remained in the City saw to it that there was money enough to distribute to the mobs when spontaneous demonstrations were desired in Cambridge or Ipswich or Canterbury or London itself; and the French Ambassador could be relied on, for strictly political reasons, to aid in fomenting and consolidating anti-Spanish feeling.

Even in a contented country, such an organization

would have been potentially formidable. Mary's religious policy of punishing the more notorious heretics by the traditional legal method of burning made it additionally so by providing occasions for public indignation which needed no factitious encouragement. Which, Elizabeth thought, was only another proof of what a fool Mary was.

Her parties at Woodstock had not, of course, been confined to political consultations and it was the last one, overmastering in its excitement, that now filled Elizabeth's mind. Cecil had brought with him a tall and handsome visitor who, he explained, was a most erudite Fellow of Trinity College, Cambridge, well versed in Greek and other learning which might edify the Princess. No obstacles had been put in the way by Bedingfield, who was not at the time aware that the twenty-seven-year-old John Dee was already recognized on the Continent as a profound practitioner of the occult arts.

Cheerfully chatting in Greek, Dee and Elizabeth, accompanied by Kate Ashley, made their way to the old summer-house in Rosamond's Bower, where the visitor cast her horoscope. He then carefully checked and counter-checked it with those of Mary and Philip and was able to announce one infallible conclusion: when Mary died she would be succeeded by Elizabeth who would have a long and glorious reign.

This was so much what Elizabeth wanted to hear that she was at first inclined to doubt it as an easy flattery and dismiss Dee as a charlatan. But his refusal to say when Mary would die or to give any information at all about her child went far to restore her faith in him, which was finally confirmed by his knowledge of certain of her past actions and by his assurance that her imprisonment at Woodstock would shortly end and that she would be summoned to Court before mid-summer—a prediction she would be able easily to verify.

To facilitate Mary's death, he gave her a small wax doll dressed as the Queen, told her to put upon it something that had belonged to Mary and instructed her how to drive, with ritual precision, a silver pin into its heart.

When they rejoined Cecil, who had more faith in political acumen than in metaphysical aid, it was decided to spread the rumor in London that the Queen had been already delivered of a boy. This would be both a convenient test of public opinion and a simple method of throwing doubt on the authenticity of the birth when it actually occurred.

And now that John Dee's first prophecy had been fulfilled and Elizabeth was indeed at Hampton Court, she had no doubt of his powers and, for the first time since her sister's accession, felt utterly secure. The terror of death at Mary's hands had gone for ever. It was Mary who would die, leaving her as Queen. She was safe. Even the fact that Dee had just been arrested on the charge of causing by witchcraft the death of one child and the blindness of another did not seriously disturb her. He equally would survive the reign and when she was Queen she would reward him as he deserved.* He had given her a new courage born of certainty of belief and, in the future, she would act on it. There was, however, no harm in using her diplomacy on Mary as long as she was alive. She continued to spend discreet time among the Popish mum-

* Ten years after these events, when she was safely on the throne, Elizabeth summoned Dee to Court to instruct her in occultism, made him her official astrologer (sending him abroad later to consult with foreign astrologers about the state of her health) and remained very much under his influence until her death.

meries in her Oratory and to attend Mass. Even if her sister did not come to see her, her piety, she knew, would be reported.

And Mary did not come. Instead, two days after her arrival, Elizabeth received a hurried note from her, saying that Philip would that afternoon be waiting on her and hoping that the warning would give her time to appear at her most becoming. Quickly she changed into her virginal dress of white satin, pearl-studded, and retired to the Oratory.

The interview with her brother-in-law, though short and formal, told her all she wanted to know. It was not Philip's words, in halting English, expressing his admiration of his "dear sister" whom he now saw for the first time; it was not the obviously learnt and rehearsed formula by which he welcomed her back to Court and promised his good offices in mediating between her and the Queen: it was his sensual lips staying a second too long on her hand and the quick, admiring glance he did not trouble to hide that convinced her that he was hers if she wanted him. Fortunately she found him not unattractive—he might even, she thought, if roused to passion, be fascinating as a lover. Should it be politic to take him from Mary, it promised to be a pleasure also. Next time—for surely he would visit her again—she would answer him a little . . .

But Philip did not return nor was she summoned for an audience with the Queen. Instead, her old enemy, the Lord Chancellor, visited her, implacable in his distrust. But this time she was not afraid, more especially as he looked so old and ill that he obviously had not long to live. With him were two Privy Councilors.

"My lords," she said, not waiting for Gardiner to speak, "I am glad to see you, for I have been kept from you for a very great while, alone in my imprisonment. You have come, I hope, to bring me tidings of release."

"As soon as you confess your faults and put yourself on the Queen's mercy," said Gardiner, "Your Highness's release will be possible."

"Rather than do that," said Elizabeth, "I will remain in prison all my life. I have never offended against my sister, the Queen, in thought, word or deed. How can I therefore ask for mercy? But I am willing, as I always have been, to be tried by justice."

That, she thought, was safe enough. Less than ever now would Mary dare bring her to trial. It would rouse the country even more than the burnings.

"You have no other word than this for Her Majesty?"

"None."

They took their leave, but next day returned with the answer.

"Your Highness," said Gardiner, "the Queen has authorized me to say that she is amazed at your boldness in refusing to confess your plottings. By your denials you make it seem as if Her Majesty has wrongly imprisoned Your Grace."

"If she believes me guilty," retorted Elizabeth, "she is surely at perfect liberty to punish me as she pleases."

"All that Her Majesty has instructed me to say is that you must tell a different tale if you wish to be released."

"Then you may tell her from me that I prefer to remain in prison in honesty than to be set free by a false confession which would confirm the Queen's unworthy suspicion of me. What I have said, I will stand to."

"In that case," said Gardiner ironically, "Your Grace

107

has the advantage of me and the Lords of the Council for your long and wrongful imprisonment."

Elizabeth flushed: "What advantage I have, you know. I have no wish to take advantage of you for having dealt with me as you have done. God forgive you!" She recollected herself in time. Fingering her rosary, she added piously: "And me also."

Gardiner looked at her with involuntary distaste as he withdrew. She felt bound to admit to herself that, whoever was deceived, he was not; nor had been from the beginning. Fortunately, now that she had Philip on her side, he was more powerless than ever.

She heard nothing more for a week. Then, at ten o'clock one night, Bedingfield knocked at her door to tell her that Mary's mistress of the robes, Catherine Pole, had come with orders to conduct her to the Queen. The summons had come at last. After two years she would be face to face with her sister again. In the falling darkness of a late May night, she went through the flower-scented gardens, accompanied by her four gentlemen with torches leading the way and her four maids of honor huddling close to her. At the foot of the private stairway to the Royal apartments, she had to dismiss them and go on alone with Bedingfield and Catherine Pole. "If I do not return, pray for me," she said, simulating a dread she did not feel, and regally mounted the stair.

When she entered the bedchamber, Mary, her body swollen, her face dank and drained of color, was sitting up in the great bed, partly shadowed by the rich hangings of crimson and gold. The arras hangings of old Flemish work depicting scenes in the life of Our Lady moved slightly— or so Elizabeth imagined—as she made her obeisance, though there was no current of air in the stifling room. As she was on her knees, she noticed the inscription on the cradle at the foot of the bed, waiting for its occupant:

> The child which Thou to Mary, O Lord of Might, has sent,
> To England's joy in health preserve, keep and defend

and comforted herself with a remembrance of John Dee's horoscope.

Without rising or waiting for the Queen to speak, she said: "God preserve Your Majesty! You will find me as true a subject to Your Majesty as any. Whatever has been reported to you, you will not find it otherwise."

"Then you will not confess," said Mary. "You stand to your truth. I pray God it may so fall out."

"If it does not, I pray for neither favor nor pardon at Your Majesty's hands."

"In that case, you insist that you have been wrongfully punished."

"I must not say so to Your Majesty," she answered, risking a half-smile.

"But you will say it to others," Mary retorted sternly. "You have said it."

"No, if it please Your Majesty. That burden I have borne and must bear alone. I humbly beseech Your Majesty ever to think of me as your true subject, not only from the beginning till now, but as long as life lasts."

"Come here, Bess," said Mary.

Elizabeth rose from her knees and went over to the bed. She was surprised how greatly Mary had aged. Mary took her face between her hands and looked searchingly into her face, screwing up her myopic eyes. Then, as if utterly tired and in despair of finding an answer, she turned away and with a great sigh murmured: "Sabe Dios." Elizabeth continued to stand there at a loss what to do or say, until the Queen turned back to her and, taking a ring from her own finger, gave it to her with: "But you can have your ring again."

Conquering her physical aversion, Elizabeth kissed her.

"Good night, Bess. Pray for me."

As soon as Elizabeth had left the room, Philip came from behind the arras.

"You heard?" said Mary.

"Of course."

"What do you think?"

"As you said, Mary. 'God knows!' But is it of much consequence now?"

"Please God, no. At last I am feeling the pains."

*THIRTEEN*

# The
# Disappointed
# Hope

*Ruy Gomez to a correspondent in Spain*
Hampton Court, June 1, 1555

. . . The Queen's deliverance keeps us all greatly exercised in our minds, although our doctors always said that the nine months are not up till June 6. She began to feel some pains yesterday . . .

*The Same to the Same*
Hampton Court, June 8, 1555

. . . The deliverance of the Queen is not expected until St. John's Day at the soonest. They say that the calculations got mixed up when they saw her with a girth greater than that of Gutierre Lopez. All this makes me doubt whether she is with child at all, greatly as I desire to see the thing happily over . . .

## The Disappointed Hope

### Simon Renard to the Emperor Charles V
Twickenham, June 24, 1555

. . . Everything in this kingdom depends on the Queen's safe deliverance. Her doctors and ladies have proved to be out in their calculations by about two months, and it now appears that she will not be delivered before about eight or ten days from now. This is the reason I have not written oftener to Your Majesty. If God is pleased to grant her a child, things will take a turn for the better. If not, I foresee trouble on so great a scale that the pen can hardly set it down. Certain it is that the order of succession has been so badly decided that the Princess Elizabeth comes next, and that means heresy again, and the true religion overthrown. Churchmen will be wronged, Catholics persecuted; there will be more acts of vengeance than heretofore and I do not know whether the King and his Court will be in safety among these people. A calamitous tragedy lies ahead. It is incredible how the delay in the Queen's deliverance encourages the heretics to slander and put about false rumours. Some say that she is not with child at all, but that a suppositious child is going to be presented as hers, and that if a suitable one had been found this already have been done. The expressions worn on people's faces are strange; folk have a more masked appearance than I have ever seen in the past. Those whom we have trusted inspire me with the most misgivings as to their loyalty. Nothing appears to be certain and I am more disturbed by what I see going on than ever before . . .

### The Same to the Same
Twickenham, June 29, 1555

. . . The Queen is as well as she has ever been during my stay in England and indeed seems to be in as good health as could be desired, so much so that one cannot doubt that she is with child. A certain sign of this is in the state of the breasts, and that the child moves. Then there is the increase of the girth, the hardening of the breasts and the fact that they distil. I trust that in ten days Your Majesty will have more certain tidings about this . . .

*Giovanni Michiel to the Doge and Senate of Venice*
Richmond, July 23, 1555

King Philip's passage across the Channel continues to be talked of and I am told on good authority that it will not be delayed beyond the 20th of next month whether the delivery takes place or not. The determination to cross without witnessing the result of the delivery seems to proceed from the Emperor's firm decision to retire to Spain, at any rate in the course of next September and King Philip's wish to confer with him before his embarkation . . .

With regard to the delivery, everyone being now of the opinion that it is unaccountably delayed, the physicians of the King and Queen and two or three of Her Majesty's most intimate female attendants, held a formal consultation last week and came, in fact, to the conclusion that they had deceived themselves by two or three months. It is undeniable and beyond a doubt, from many manifest signs, that the Queen is pregnant, but not so far gone as was believed and published at the time . . .

*Queen Mary to the Emperor Charles V*
(*written in her own hand*)

My lord and good father, I have learnt by what the King my Lord and good husband has told me and also by the letter that you were pleased to send me that for a long time past the state of your affairs has demanded that Your Majesty and he should meet in order to confer together and reach appropriate decisions. However, you have been pleased to put off the moment of separating him from me until now, for which I very humbly thank Your Majesty.

I assure you, Sire, that there is nothing in this world that I set so much store by as the King's presence; but, as I have more concern for Your Majesty's welfare than for my own desires, I submit to what you regard as necessary.

I firmly hope that the King's absence will be brief, for I assure Your Majesty that, quite apart from my own feelings, his presence in this kingdom has done much good and is of great importance for the good governance of this country.

### *Giovanni Michiel to the Doge and Senate of Venice*
Richmond, August 5, 1555

Their Majesties, three days ago, proceeded to the little village of Oatlands, four miles farther from London, not merely to give the opportunity for the cleansing of Hampton Court, where they have remained so long a while, but on another more important account and perhaps a more necessary one, which, although no one dares to proclaim it, is nevertheless tacitly understood by everybody.

The fact is that the move has been made in order no longer to keep the people of England in suspense about this delivery by the constant and public processions that were made and by the Queen's remaining so many days in retirement. Not only did she not transact any business, but she would scarcely allow herself to be seen by any but the ladies who, in expectation of this childbirth, had flocked to Court from all parts of the kingdom in such numbers (all living at the cost of Her Majesty!) that Hampton Court, though one of the largest palaces to be seen here or anywhere else, could hardly contain them. By this change of residence, an opportunity is provided with dispensing with the processions without any scandal and for the Queen to free herself from expense by letting most of these ladies return to their homes, on the excuse of the limited accommodation at Oatlands.

By this release, without proceeding to any formal announcement, all persons may clearly realise that the hope of childbirth has so diminished that but little reliance may now be placed on it. The chief personages here, perceiving that Her Majesty's belly did not increase but rather diminished, have come to the conclusion that the pregnancy will end in wind rather than anything else, although it is said, for the sake of keeping the populace in hope and consequently in check, that the Queen is in her sixth or seventh month. But the result of this rumour will soon be cleared up as it is not a thing that can be long concealed . . .

On the Queen's departure, leave was given to the Lady Elizabeth to withdraw with all her attendants to a house distant three miles from Her Majesty's; and on the Queen's expected return to Hampton Court in eight or ten days, it is supposed that Elizabeth will not come back, but either remain where she is or go to another of her palaces, as she is completely free.

*The Same to the Same*
Richmond, August 19, 1555

Last week Their Majesties returned to Hampton Court, the Lady Elizabeth remaining at the seat to which she went; and now the Queen shows herself and converses with everybody as usual. Her health is so good as perhaps never to have been better, to the universal surprise of all who see her. Of delivery of pregnancy small signs are visible externally and no one talks or thinks of it any longer.

As to the King's departure, it is said that he will leave in eight or ten days, leaving the greater part of his household for the sake of convincing the Queen, by as many signs as he can, that he intends to return speedily. But the contrary is rumoured more than ever and it is said that he will go to Spain and by degrees remove his household and all others from England.

### The Same to the Same
London, September 3, 1555

On the 29th ult., the King left Greenwich. Much to my pleasure, I accompanied Cardinal Pole and the other noblemen when they went with the King to his barge to see him take leave of the Queen. Though evidently deeply grieved in her heart, she chose to come with him through all the chambers and galleries to the head of the stairs, forcing herself the whole way to avoid, in sight of such a crowd, any demonstration unbecoming her regal dignity.

On returning, however, to her apartments, she placed herself at a window which looks on the river and, not supposing herself to be seen or observed by anyone, it was perceived she gave free vent to her grief by a flood of tears. Nor did she once move from the window until she had not only seen the King embark and depart but remained looking after him as long as he was in sight.

The King, on his part, mounted aloft on the barge in

order to be better seen as it approached in sight of the window, waved his bonnet to salute her, demonstrating great affection.

Shortly before he departed, the King sent for Cardinal Pole and all the Lords of the Council and commended the government of the kingdom to them in his absence. Turning towards Cardinal Pole, he besought him very earnestly in his own name and that of the Queen to assume this charge, in conformity with his own patriotism and the wish of Their Majesties, desiring all others to defer to him in everything. Henceforth, therefore, all public and important business will be discussed and decided according to the opinion and advice of his right reverend Lordship.

### Cardinal Pole to King Philip
#### Greenwich, September 16, 1555

As nothing can be more agreeable to me than to obey the commands of Your Majesty on your departure, I am informing Your Majesty that the Queen passes the morning in prayer, after the manner of Mary, and in the afternoon admirably personates Martha by transacting business; so urging her councillors as to keep them all incessantly occupied. In this way she mitigates her grief for Your Majesty's absence, imagining you present in their persons. Her chief consolation is the hope of your return, for which daily prayers are made by her . . .

### The Emperor Charles V to his daughter,
### the Regent of Spain
#### Brussels, September 23, 1555

. . . The Queen of England's deliverance is being so much delayed that it makes us doubt; for now they are trying to tell us that she became pregnant many days later than was assumed on the first count. Well, we must accept God's will, whatever it may be! . . .

> ### *The King of the Romans' Ambassador to the King of the Romans*
> Brussels, September 29, 1555

. . . As there is no hope of fruit from the English marriage, discussions are going on everywhere about the consort to be given to Elizabeth who is and will continue to be lawful heir unless the King and Queen have issue . . .

# FOURTEEN

# A
# Husband for
# Elizabeth

THE CONSORT whom, from the beginning,
Philip wished to be given to Elizabeth was Emmanuel
Philibert, Duke of Savoy and Prince of Piedmont, already
at twenty-five, a brilliant soldier, whose audacious courage was to win for him the nickname "Ironhead." He was
Philip's first cousin—their mothers were sisters—but, in
their mutual affection, they seemed brothers. One of
Philip's first actions after his marriage had been to arrange
for Savoy to visit England. The young Duke had been
elected Knight of the Garter and the insignia taken to him,
by an eminent embassy, at his headquarters in Flanders.
Somerset House, Elizabeth's town residence, had been
ordered to be placed at his disposal whenever he should
arrive. And as if to emphasize the importance of it the
King of France had instructed his ambassador in England
that the prevention of the marriage was a political priority

which demanded that he should use every possible means to hinder a match between Elizabeth and Savoy, "poor and dispossessed as he is."

The French concern was due to more than the fact that the marriage, should it be arranged, would deprive them of Elizabeth as a tool and would commit England unbreakably to the Spanish-Imperial *bloc*. Military considerations were also involved in it. Savoy was "poor and dispossessed" only because the French had dispossessed him. His duchy was essential to France as the highway for its armies invading Italy and as a buffer against Imperial counter-attack. Emmanuel Philibert in command of one of the Imperial armies had no other aim than to rescue his people from the grinding oppression of French occupation. Their continual and piteous appeals gave an edge even to his own unresting attack, and whenever peace between the great powers was discussed, he fought by diplomacy as tenaciously as by war.

Of all the Imperial leaders he was the one most feared by the French and when news arrived that he was at last to visit England, the King of France had ordered 15,000 men in seventeen ships to intercept and capture him. He had been saved only by a sudden change of wind blowing him out of his course which ensured that though the Calais-Dover crossing took him twenty hours it was accomplished in safety.

When news of the landing reached London, de Noailles had torn out his beard with rage and disappointment. He felt that his responsibility now became acute. He had found, however, an unexpected ally in the Queen herself. For Mary had refused, despite all Philip could say or do, to allow Elizabeth and Savoy to meet. She herself had been charming to him. He had been entertained, fêted, honored, consulted, but he was not permitted to see the Princess. No one had been able to understand the Queen's reasons. In vain had Philip urged that the Savoy marriage was the best that could be devised; that his cousin's lineage was among the proudest in Europe, far beyond anything to which the daughter of Anne Boleyn might have hoped to aspire; that he was an eminently personable young man; that his devotion to the Catholic cause was unquestioned; that the people of England, who might have resented Elizabeth marrying a German or a Spaniard, would be likely to approve the match; that, if Savoy did not marry England, he might be tempted to marry France, with unpredictable diplomatic consequences; and that, by ensuring Elizabeth's departure from England, the marriage might calm the situation at home.

Admitting it all—for the arguments were too cogent to disallow—Mary had answered, immovably, "No," and Emmanuel Philibert had left again for the wars as far from marriage with the forbidden Princess as on his storm-tossed entry.

And now, in Brussels, in those early October days of 1555, the matter was being once more discussed with urgency. As Philip had feared, the French, having failed to seize the young man by force, were trying to entangle him by marriage and offering him the restoration of Savoy and part of Piedmont as a wedding-present if he would become the husband of the Princess Margaret of France. There was little danger that he would accept, but even the possibility increased Philip's irritation with Mary for her continued refusal.

"I shall prevail upon her," he assured Emmanuel Philibert. "If she does not consent, I shall not return to England."

"You must not make me the excuse for that," retorted his cousin, "leave it to time."

To counterbalance what Philip continued to regard as an insult, Savoy was given every mark of honor at the Court at Brussels. At the great ceremony when the Emperor formally abdicated in favor of Philip, he was seated on Charles's left hand and it was noticed that he alone did not uncover. And he retained his soldier's impassivity as a wave of emotion engulfed the assembly.

Charles recounted how he had been called to the Crown of Spain when he was sixteen and the Imperial Crown when he was nineteen; how, for thirty-five years he had discharged his responsibilities, traveling nine times to Germany, six to Spain, seven to Italy, France four times, Africa twice and England twice, apart from his ten visits to Brussels itself. "Of all the wars I waged," he said, "some were for the defense of the Faith, some for the defense of my rights, others were for the cause of justice which the Imperial Crown upholds; but I have waged no war from ambition or hatred." Now the time had come for him to prepare in solitude in a monastery, to face the judgment of the King of Kings, and to leave to his son and his brother the continuance of the struggle in the world.

"Never let this one thing out of your minds," he concluded: "the purity of our Catholic religion, over which you will have to watch as over an exceptionally important fortress surrounded by hostile armies. If the enemy has perchance sown tares among your land, pull them out; pull them out by the roots before it is too late, for otherwise—you will remember my words—you will become in misery slaves to your errors, without the power to set yourselves free when you wish it. I tell you, I would rather have lost what I was and what I had—I would rather lose what I am—than accept the least error as regards the purity of Christ's commands."

He turned to Philip, who rose from his seat, cap in hand and knelt before him. He implored him, this time with a personal intensity, above all things to safeguard the Faith. Neither father nor son made any attempt to check their tears as Philip solemnly promised and Charles gave him his blessing. Sobs were heard from all parts of the hall. But Savoy, without any change of countenance gazed at his cousin hoping he had counted the cost of his promise in terms of war to the death. Philip, he had to admit, was no soldier as his father had been and, in reaction from the stress of his correctitude in England, he was now allowing himself to become immersed in soft delights. It was, he thought, understandable, though everyone deplored it and, with couriers arriving almost every day from England, it was impossible that Mary should not hear of it and further harden her heart . . .

The stars in their courses seemed to be fighting against Mary. Continuous rains and floods made that autumn of 1555 memorable as the worst ever known in England. That Westminster Hall itself was under six feet of water so that wherries could sail in it was a minor inconvenience in comparison with the disaster of the destruction of all the crops, which made bread five times its usual price. The hay-harvest was swamped and three-quarters of the country's cattle died. Faced with the impossibility of taxing a starving people, the Queen appealed to her nobility to repay some of the arrears of their debts to the Crown—there was hardly one who did not owe her £5,000 and most were her debtors for £8,000—only to be told that they would not pay her a halfpenny until she had first

123

taken back from the Church the stolen property and revenues she had recently restored to it.

Discontent, focused unfalteringly on her religion by the Protestant-paid mischief-makers, rose to such heights that two attempts were made to assassinate her—one by the gunner of a ship passing Greenwich where she was in residence, who fired, under the pretence of a salute, a small cannon directly into the Royal Apartment, the other, by a dagger during the session of Parliament which she twice attended.

Personal danger to herself she had never troubled about and half contemptuously pardoned the gunner on his plea that it was an "accident." It was the political danger that oppressed her. At the opening of Parliament, Gardiner, with mortal sickness already on him, made his last and greatest speech appealing for loyalty and faith to men who had neither. Then he went home to die, leaving Mary bereft of her shrewdest and wisest counselor. Even Pole, because of his long years of exile, was no substitute for one who had so certainly the English touch and who knew, from years of proximity, the degrees of treachery by which she was surrounded, and the best way of meeting them.

To make matters worse, the new Pope, Paul IV, was at odds with both Pole and Philip. An eighty-five-year-old fanatic who reintroduced the Inquisition to Rome and founded the Index, he opposed not only the least concession to the Protestants but even reasonable argument with them. Of the situation in England he had less than no comprehension and Pole's charity and tolerance seemed to him evidence that the Cardinal himself must be secretely a heretic. For Spain he, an Italian of the Italians, had an obsessive hatred so great that it became a monomania. He would not even receive his own nephews until they gave some evidence that they shared it. To him the Spaniards were barbarians to be destroyed and Charles and Philip the enemies, not the champions of the Faith. He announced: "We shall declare a crusade against them so that the Emperor may see the annihilation of this damnable race in his lifetime." And, to give point to the threat, he allied himself with France to compass the downfall of Philip.

Mary, sharing her husband's unpopularity, wanted only the solace of his presence and found the days of separation increasingly difficult to endure. For some weeks she was buoyed by the promise that Charles himself would visit her on his way back to Spain. She had Dover Castle prepared as a residence for him and thirty ships manned and kept in readiness to escort him across the Channel. But he did not come and Philip wrote to explain that political necessities detained them both a little longer in the Low Countries. He also requested that those of his household who had remained in England should join him, explaining that, in the circumstances, he could no longer avail himself of his father's suite. Mary tried to believe him, but no one else did and when all had gone but his confessor, the Franciscan, Alfonso de Castro, even she gave way in misery to an uncontrollable anger and had his portrait removed from the Privy Chamber.

Philip, hearing of it, promised to return by Christmas, but a fortnight later changed it to the Epiphany. By mid-December, it became "as soon as possible" and before Christmas he recalled even de Castro.

On his arrival in Brussels, the friar remonstrated with him:

"Her Majesty thinks that my recall means that you will

never return to her. She is ill at the prospect of it. She has aged ten years in three months."

"Even my affection for her," said Philip, "cannot make me abandon my duty here. I, too, am not in full health."

The friar looked at him sourly, for Philip's illness was only too palpably the result of his continuous debaucheries, but he checked his intended retort and said quietly: "Her Majesty considers that your first duty is to give England an heir. Without that there is no safety for anyone."

Philip laughed unkindly. "Then let her marry Elizabeth to Savoy," he said. "That would be a surer move than my bedding with her again."

"I urged it on her, as you ordered, not once but several times. I even strained my theology to make her obedience to you in that come within the marriage oath. But she would have none of it."

"What reason did she give?"

"None—though she said she would never force her sister against her will and that Elizabeth would not hear of it."

"Of course Elizabeth would not hear of it; France would see to that," Philip flung at him, as if he were to blame. "But Mary must have some reason. Or does she now want to play France's game, like the Pope?"

"I am sure it is not that, sir. She is devoted to you body and soul."

"Where is Elizabeth?" said Philip suddenly.

"In her country house at Hatfield. She was with the Queen at Greenwich until the opening of Parliament. After that Her Majesty allowed her to go where she wished."

"You noticed nothing strange between them?"

"No." The friar hesitated. "There was one matter which caused much comment but it did not affect the Queen."

"What was it?"

"Cardinal Pole, whose apartments at Greenwich were near Elizabeth's, took care never to see her."

"Why?"

"I cannot tell you. I was not in the Cardinal's confidence. But it was put down to the scrupulosity of his loyalty to Her Majesty."

Whether or not de Castro stressed the last words, Philip affected to think that he did and took it as a further reproach.

"It may be that Mary should have married that thin old man—though there'd have been no children that way either—but it was ordered otherwise. And, as I'm her husband, by God she shall obey me and give her sister to Savoy. Or never see me again."

"I will wait," said de Castro, "till you are in better mind and health," and withdrew to say a prayer for the Queen of England.

# FIFTEEN

# Conspiracy

Eʟɪᴢᴀʙᴇᴛʜ, sᴇᴄᴜʀᴇ at Hatfield under the amiable surveillance of Sir Thomas Pope, who was no Bedingfield, decided that the time was at last propitious for unseating her sister. Mary was ill; her vexation at Philip's tardiness made her more than ever liable to misjudge events and, further sapping her certainty, was the knowledge of Europe's laughter at her imagined pregnancy. Her dignity was corroded and, like a wounded animal, she hid herself from the world. This made it the easier to spread rumors that she was, if not actually dead, at least mortally ill. Men's eyes were turning to Elizabeth. When she set out for Hatfield, so de Noailles informed his master, "great and small followed her through the City and greeted her with acclamations and such vehement manifestations of affection that she was afraid it would expose her to the jealousy of the Court and, with her usual caution, she fell back behind some of the officers of her train as if unwilling to attract public attention and applause."

Elizabeth was not on this occasion merely acting. She

was genuinely alarmed. The comparison with the misery and fear of her last public progress through London only eighteen months before was too remarkable. The last thing she wanted was a triumph with the unstable London mob which, by exacerbating Mary, might make it more difficult for her to achieve the reality of power. Gratifying as it was that she need no longer fear the Queen, it would have been madness to allow the appearance of rivalry.

Once safely at Hatfield, however, she lost no time. Kate Ashley was there; and the Parrys. Cecil paid his usual visits. Roger Ascham, ostensibly instructing her in the classics, was a new link with the Protestant plotters abroad—"I teach her words," as he put it, "and she me things"—and her Italian master, Battista Castiglione, was invaluable as an additional liaison with London. On his visits to the city to buy lute strings for her or take a book to the bookbinders, he could call unsuspected at the French Embassy, visit Somerset House, where the seditious pamphlets printed abroad were stored in ever greater numbers, and look in at "Arundel's" in Lawrence Poulteney Lane which was the resort of the young Protestant Members of Parliament organizing opposition to the Queen's policy.

Even more important was young Henry Peckham, a member of her household, whose father, Sir Edmund, was one of Mary's Privy Councilors and her trusty and trustworthy Master of the Mint. Through the son, unsuspected by his father, Elizabeth could obtain access to official documents and secrets possible in no other way.

Henry Peckham's usefulness, however, went even beyond abstracting Henry VIII's will from the Rolls and advising on the most effective way to rob the Mint. He was also the center of a wealthy, discontented group of young men in their twenties who were willing to devote both their property and their tongues to treason. Among them was Christopher Ashton, whose house on the London road near Abingdon was a convenient meeting place for them and who could also be relied on to explain to his friends that "the Lady Elizabeth is a jolly, liberal dame and nothing so unthankful as her sister is." This liberality she inherited from her mother "who was one of the bountifullest women of all her time or since."

The friends of Anne Boleyn were, in fact, at key points of the plot. They could be trusted. Sir Richard Uvedale, the Governor of the Isle of Wight who had undertaken to deliver the Island to the French and to spike the guns of Portsmouth to facilitate their invasion of the mainland, was the son of Anne Boleyn's secretary. John Throgmorton, the energetic organizer of the conspiracy and, by reason of his courage, its real leader, had been brought up in the household of Anne Boleyn's uncle. Sir Anthony Kingston, Member of Parliament for Gloucestershire and Provost Marshal for Cornwall, who was to raise the West, was the son of that Sir William Kingston who had been Governor of the Tower of London during Anne Boleyn's last imprisonment and, as a boy of sixteen, he had fallen under the spell of her fateful beauty.

The cornerstone of the plan was, as on the previous occasion, the marriage of Elizabeth to her cousin Edward Courtenay and her proclamation as Queen after Mary had been murdered in the insurrection, during which the Mint was to be plundered and London to be set on fire in various places by way of diversion. Courtenay at the moment was abroad and Elizabeth herself would have preferred to have joined him in France and come back to

England at the head of a French army in the guise of a liberator from Spanish tyranny.

The French King, however, who was financing the project, was aghast at such romanticism and de Noailles received a peremptory order: "Above all, see that Madame Elizabeth makes no move of any sort or kind to undertake the thing you wrote of, for that would ruin all." The Princess's part, until the hour struck, was to present at Hatfield a picture of charming and persecuted innocence, leaving the French action and diplomacy in the capable hands of Sir Henry Dudley, who was experienced in these particular matters.

In the previous reign Dudley had been Admiral of the Narrow Seas and Captain of Guard at Guisnes. When Edward VI died and Sir Henry's cousin, the Duke of Northumberland, tried to exclude Mary from the throne in favor of his daughter-in-law, Lady Jane Grey, his part had been to offer to betray Calais to the French in return for their support in the English insurrection. Mary, with England behind her, had defeated that attempt, but in the three years which had elapsed since then, Calais, the last and much prized English possession in France, had become infested by Protestant "exiles." In an enthusiasm of treason, they would certainly facilitate its handing-over and so have brought the matter again into the realm of practical politics. That Mary had both pardoned him and actually paid his debts weighed nothing with Dudley, an ambitious swashbuckler who, tormented with delusions of grandeur, saw himself as the new arbiter of England's destiny.

Other members of the conspiracy had been selected from various strata of society on the score of their usefulness. There was the Keeper of the Star Chamber who had a house by the river's edge where the gold stolen from the Mint could be hidden until it was safe to transport it to the Isle of Wight; there was an expert maker of skeleton keys; there was a coiner; and there was an obliging young man whose rôle was to impersonate the dead Edward VI, after the countryside had been flooded with pamphlets, informing the people that the King was in fact alive and well in France and only awaiting a loyal demonstration in his favor to enable him to come and recover the crown.

As a *ballon d'essai*, this was ingenious but disappointing. The response was negligible. The youth was captured and hanged. The conspirators, unsuspected at being involved in what appeared to be an independent lunacy, realized that the time was not yet ripe and Elizabeth made haste to give evidence of the exclusively artistic nature of her pursuits by staging an elaborate masque, banquet and play at Hatfield. She also invited Mary down to visit her and, after Mass, at which the Queen was able to witness her sister's new-found devotion to Catholicism, she provided a concert in which she herself played the virginals, accompanied by a chorister with "a divine voice." Mary was impressed.

Whether or not suspicion was satisfactorily allayed, Cecil at least thought it prudent to provide some evidence of his own devout Catholicism and wrote to Pole requesting that, as he had always had a "natural horror" of fish, he might "for the quietening of his conscience" have a dispensation to eat meat in Lent, Fridays and Saturdays excepted. Pole granted it.

It was Pole's nature to trust men until he had reason to do otherwise, as it was Cecil's to doubt them in all circumstances. Thus both saw in others reflections of their own characters and though it was generally agreed that Cecil's was more suitable for a statesman, the Cardinal, merely by reason of the simplicity of his goodness, had his own occasional triumphs. He had one now. One of the conspirators, stricken by conscience, sought audience with him and gave him such details of the plot as he knew. Pole informed the Council and took the precaution of removing the gold from the Mint. The Queen's guard was doubled and scrutinized for loyalty and Mary herself wrote to Philip more urgently than usual to return to England—which, as usual, he promised but did not perform. They then waited for the conspirators to make the first move.

This was precipitated, unexpectedly, by the comet. At the beginning of March, a "blazing star" suddenly appeared in the heavens and remained there for a fortnight. The phenomenon was sufficiently curious to cause superstitious alarm, which the conspirators turned to their own purposes. Picked preachers went about London proclaiming that it heralded the Day of Judgment and that shortly everything would be consumed by fire from Heaven. This, they thought, would increase the effectiveness, as agents of panic, of the various fires which they intended to kindle as a signal for the assault on the Mint and the Palace and the murder of the Queen. Unfortunately, a gang of rogues unconnected with the plot thought of the same plan to cover their own independent series of robberies; and in the ensuing confusion the conspirators were forced to come into the open before they had intended and the government to strike before they could capture them all. "Had the Council delayed for two or three days," the Venetian Ambassador reported, "they would have captured the whole gang." As it was, Sir

Henry Dudley escaped to France and Sir Anthony Kingston committed suicide on his way up to London. But Throgmorton and Peckham were among those taken.

Mary, whose courage had risen to meet the crisis, was, in the reaction of safety after the arrests, at the edge of despair. For nights she had not slept and her wakefulness was haunted by an endless vista of treachery and hatred, worse than the worst dream. In the labyrinth of disloyalty and loneliness, she turned to Pole in something not far from panic and forbade him to leave her side.

The first arrests had been made on Wednesday, March 18. The following Sunday was Passion Sunday on which the Cardinal had arranged to go to Canterbury for his consecration as Archbishop in succession to Thomas Cranmer who a month before had been degraded for heresy from that office by the Pope.

"You must not leave Greenwich, Reynald," Mary told Pole. "They will find means to assassinate you on the journey."

"I have lived with that likelihood for twenty years," he answered, "and it disturbs me now less than ever."

Her deep voice became suddenly shrill: "No, Reynald, no. I ask this for myself. I cannot be left alone. If Philip were here, I would not ask it. But now you must stay with me. You must stay with me."

"As you wish, Mary."

"The consecration can be here at Greenwich. In Greyfriars. And your priesting, too. Nothing need be altered, except that it is here." Then, quietly, she added: "And I can be at your first Mass."

They looked at one another, each realizing the implications of that moment. Pole, obsessed always by fears of his own unworthiness for the supreme office of the priest-

135

hood, had intended to die in deacon's orders; and it had only been at Mary's urgent entreaty that he had reluctantly allowed himself to be nominated for the vacant archbishopric of Canterbury. Politically, he saw the force of her argument. As Legate, he was the obvious choice for the Primacy. Had he already been a priest, he would not have hesitated. The Primacy in itself did not disturb him—it was hardly more than a secular necessity of little spiritual importance. But before he could become Primate, he must be priested. It was that he feared. The echo of his conversation with Mary, when at last she had persuaded him, came back to them both now.

He had pleaded his own unworthiness only to be answered by: "Yet you ask worthiness from others. Reynald, pay God what you owe. Why do you hesitate?"

"I have told you, Mary—my unworthiness. I *do* fear it," he had answered. "It's the final, secret fear. I can say this only to you. You and I kneel together at Mass. Let me remain on my knees."

"Refuse the privilege to stand and sacrifice?"

"I cannot refuse what, I think, has not been offered. That's it, Mary. Christ's words to His apostles: 'You have not chosen me, but I have chosen you.' No man can choose the priesthood. He is chosen. And if he usurps the choice, he risks damnation."

"Cranmer's a priest."

It had been shrewd of Mary to counter in this way, but Pole had been unshaken in his quiet answer: "I judge no one, but it may be that our times will be known as 'the age of unworthy priests.' Let me, at least, knowing my frailty, remain a deacon."

But Mary had persisted: "Would you know if you had been chosen?"

136

"I think so."

"Your conscience?"

"That—and outward things."

"You fear the burden of Canterbury?"

Pole had looked at her incredulously. "You cannot think that. I'm Legate, harder worked than any Archbishop. No. Pope and Archbishops are priests. To me that's all they are. There's nothing more to be. But it is not for me."

Mary had caught at the mention of the Pope. "Make one test of your private fear. You owe that to God. Let the Pope choose for you."

"Caraffa?" Pole had been certain that, in the circumstances, he would be the last person the new Pope would appoint Primate of all England.

"Yes. Caraffa. If he approves you, there's your call."

So it had been left, and against all probability the Pope had approved it.

But Pole's priesting, now two days away, had another implication. Neither could forget that, even more than Mary's marriage to Philip, Pole's ordination would be the final destruction of their mothers' dreams; and, with the irony of a final paradox, it came at the time when Pole was in fact fulfilling the functions of a king and governing where Philip had virtually abdicated. Now, in another way, he would come nearer to her.

She would be at his first Mass; receive on her tongue from his hand the Body of God when first he, in humble fear, exercised his privilege of consecrating It. He, who could not be King, must more than ever continue to rule. He, who could not be husband, must now be confessor and spiritual father.

"You will not leave me, Reynald?" She was calm now.

"No, Mary. Never."

In her matter-of-fact, bustling way, she came back to the ordinary plane of everyday reality and took up the burden of ruling.

"Where does Cranmer stand in this plot?"

"There's no way of telling; but it's of no consequence now, I think."

They had no doubt that Cranmer, under house-arrest at Oxford since his degradation from the Archbishopric, must have known that the conspiracy was afoot. Ashton's house near Abingdon was only a few miles away; Elizabeth had kept in touch with Oxford, and access to Cranmer through common friends was easy enough. Nevertheless it was to the highest degree unlikely that he had made any personal move. His essay in high treason at the beginning of the reign made him afraid of more. What now assumed a different significance in Pole's eyes was the request Cranmer had made for a personal disputation with him on theological matters. As the two men had known and argued with each other since the days when Henry VIII had first attempted to rid himself of Catherine of Aragon, the suggestion could only be construed as an effort to play for time. Time for what? At last Pole knew.

Not until that very Wednesday when the first arrests were made did Cranmer write his seventh and final recantation. Pole now showed it to Mary. In it the one-time Archbishop confessed that he had sinned against Heaven and against the realm of England; that, as the cause and the author of the divorce of Henry VIII, he deserved both temporal and eternal punishment for it, because from that divorce had sprung, as from a seed, the deaths of many good men, the schism of the realm and havoc beyond imagination. He admitted that he had opened the windows of all the heresies, especially on the sacrament of the Holy Eucharist. He had done more damage to the Christian religion than Saul the persecutor . . .

Mary, reading it, said: "He has told the truth at last. I pray God may have mercy on him for what he has done."

But, in the circumstances, there could be no temporal mercy. At any other time, it might have been possible, after his public and seven times reiterated penitence, to have allowed him to live the rest of his life out quietly in one of the refounded monasteries, practicing the religion in which he had been brought up and to which, after his great betrayal, he had now returned. That was what Cranmer himself envisaged. That was what Pole had assumed in the long letter he had written to him earlier in the year which ended: "You have not, like others, fallen through simplicity or through fear. You were corrupted like the Jews, by earthly rewards and promises. For your own profit you denied the Presence of your Lord and you rebelled against His servant, the Pope. May you see your crimes. May you feel the greatness of your need of mercy. Now, even now, by my mouth, Christ offers you that mercy; and with the passionate hope which I am bound to feel for your salvation, I wait your answer to your Master's call."

By custom, now that Cranmer had made public recantation of his heresies, the temporal punishment of death by fire should be remitted. Moreover, there seemed no doubt of the sincerity of the fallen Archbishop's return to the Faith. He had made his private confession and received absolution; for the young Dominican, Fray Juan de Garcia, who lived in his company and discussed theology with him, he had developed a deep affection; he had asked for Thomas More's *Comfort Against Tribulation* and in those writings of the man who had preferred to die a martyr's death rather than accept the result of Cranmer's actions, he found comfort indeed. He attended Mass, received the Sacrament and repeated continuously those Litanies, with their invocations to the saints, which he himself had once banished from the life of England. Why should such a man die? To send him to the fire seemed not only unjust but impolitic, for his case was palpably different from that of the Protestant Bishops Ridley and Latimer, who had died because they persisted in their heresy.

So Pole and Mary argued, trying to escape the imperative of the moment. But the moment tyrannized unmercifully. The practical had ousted the theoretical. Had the plot succeeded, Cranmer would now have been free. He would have been once more Archbishop, hero of a Protestant triumph, able to reject his recantation contemptuously as something forced upon him and to destroy the evidence of it as if it had never been. Nor was there any assurance that, even now, the conspiracy was foiled. No one knew, or for months would know, how wide or how deep was the treason; and, at such a moment, to spare Cranmer would be taken not for mercy but for weakness, not only by the English Protestants but by the French King. Whatever Pole or Mary might personally have wished, however the withholding of pardon from a repentant heretic might be criticized, there was no course compatible with the responsibility of government but his death.

Once the decision was taken, they acted with unyielding haste. Dr. Henry Cole, a lawyer, Provost of Eton and Canon of Westminister, a friend of both Cranmer and Pole, was sent for and ordered to ride immediately to Oxford to inform Cranmer that he must die that Saturday. Before the execution, Cole was to preach a public sermon, explaining the reason for it, so that, as far as possible, the populace should understand the unexpected action. Mary herself gave Cole the heads of that discourse. He was to die, in spite of his reconciliation, because by his conduct in usurping the Pope's authority and, pronouncing the divorce of Henry VIII, he had been the cause of the many evils which had followed. He was to die because he had continued so long in his heresy, debating and defending it till the last moment, so that to pardon him would set a precedent, since "it had never been seen in the time of schism that any man continuing so long had been pardoned." And, finally, he was to die because the Queen and Council had their own good reasons "which were not meet and convenient for everyone to understand."

"With respect," said Cole who, knowing of the discovery of the plot, understood the reasons perfectly, "will not this rouse curiosity and set tongues wagging, where silence would be better?"

"We have considered that," said Pole, "but there is one man who will understand it. If Cranmer has any part in this plot, he will know what we know. Let us pray God he is sincere in his repentance."

When, on Friday evening, Cole saw Cranmer, his first question was whether he was continuing firmly in the Faith. Cranmer said that he was and, with tears in his eyes asked Cole to use his good offices with Mary on behalf of his young son, who, by his death, would be left an orphan. Cole promised and, finding his task easier because of Cranmer's assumption that he was to die, they talked of death quietly, as one priest to another. Cranmer said that

141

he had no fear of it, except for the burden on his conscience, and told Cole of the various Requiem Masses which he had requested to be said for the repose of his soul.

They discussed the arrangements for the morrow—Cranmer's public recantation of his heresies in the terms which he had privately sent on the Wednesday to Mary and Pole; Cole's sermon in which he promised to charge every priest to say a Mass for him; the conduct of the execution. Cole would visit him again privately in the morning, but Cranmer asked that it should not be until after Fray Juan de Garcia had heard his last confession and given him his final absolution.

Yet though it might seem that Cole had fulfilled his responsibility and that Cranmer had accepted his fate, the matter was, in fact, left in uncertainty. That the stake should be prepared and the procedure of death enacted was the convention of a public "Act of Faith" which Cranmer, in common with everyone else, assumed. But within that convention came also the reprieve, unpromised but expected; nor did Cranmer seriously doubt that by the terms of his recantation he would earn it. Though he was prepared for death, he was not expecting it.*

So it was not until next morning, as he listened to Cole's sermon in St. Mary's and realized the implications of it, that he knew that all hope of life was at an end. Men noticed that during the discourse, he was laboring under an intense emotion, though they ascribed it wrongly. It was not penitence which was shaking him, but uncontrollable anger. If he was to die in any case—and Cole's

---

* Foxe affirmed that Cole never told Cranmer he was to die, but later historians have suggested that, though informed, he was assuming a reprieve.

reference to the secret "good reasons of the Queen and Council" made the situation quite clear to him—he would die like Samson, pulling down the house on his enemies, and involving them in his own destruction.

The time came for him to read his recantation which he had carefully written out so that there should be no unwitting mistake in it. The final sentence was: "And now I come to the great thing that so troubles my conscience more than anything that ever I did or said in my life; and that is the setting abroad untrue books and writings contrary to the truth of God's word—the books which I wrote against the Sacrament of the Altar since the death of King Henry VIII."

As he started this, he continued to read in his even voice he had used for the earlier sections: "And now I come to the great thing that so troubles my conscience more than anything that ever I did or said in my life and that is the setting abroad . . ." But then he paused, put down his manuscript and in a voice that vibrated to every corner of the church, continued passionately: ". . . the setting abroad of writings contrary to the truth; which now here I renounce and refuse as things written with my hand contrary to the truth which I thought in my heart; and wrote for fear of death and to save my life, if it might be; and that is, all such documents as I have written or signed with my own hand since my degradation. In them I have written many untrue things. And forasmuch as my hand offended in writing contrary to my heart, therefore my hand shall first be punished. For, if I come to the fire, it shall be first burned. And, as for the Pope, I refuse him, as Christ's enemy and anti-Christ, with all his false doctrine."

Pandemonium broke out as, recanting his recantation,

he was led to the stake. But, overtopping the hubbub, ignoring the cries of anger and surprise from the crowds, Fray Juan de Garcia argued imploringly with him not thus to risk his salvation.

"Do not die so desperately," he pleaded. "Recollect yourself. Remember your confession a few hours ago."

Cranmer, deliberately affecting to misunderstand the point of his plea, said: "Well, and is not confession a good thing?"

"Then how can you die unreconciled?"

Cranmer was uneasy. To escape his friend's importunity, he turned to those in the crowd whom he knew to be Protestants and shouted: "This fellow would have me take the Pope for the Head of the Church, when he is its tyrant."

Fray Juan fell back on a desperate retort: "Certainly you would have acknowledged him Head if he had spared *your* head."

There was a moment of tense silence as the two men looked into each other's eyes for the last time. Then the surprised bystanders heard Cranmer calmly acknowledge it. "Of course. If he had saved me alive, I should have obeyed his laws."

There was nothing more to be said. Fray Juan ceased arguing, but spent what was left of the time in importunate prayers that, even if it were delayed till the last second of life, grace might still triumph in the dying man's soul. But all that was seen by the crowd at the stake was that gesture which was to live through history—Cranmer's thrusting first into the flames the hand which had signed his recantations and calling out with a loud voice: "This hand has offended." After which he spoke no more . . .

Mary and Pole, when Cole returned to Greenwich and

reported the circumstances to them, had no doubt of the consequences of that dying protest. It would give, at this moment of danger, a rallying-cry and a watchword to the forces of discontent. Cranmer's careful choice of "if" rather than "when" in referring at that point to his inescapable death even suggested that his speech had been planned for the purpose of rousing Oxford to an attempted rescue. But, in any case, the very thing they had sought to avoid they had precipitated. Cranmer dead had given a new cutting-edge to the blunted forces of the conspiracy and they realized that it was impossible for a moment to relax their interrogations of the arrested plotters. Though Holy Week had begun, this time the clemency of two years ago was out of the question.

Yet, in spite of the renewed danger of assassination, Mary refused to abandon her public duties on Maundy Thursday. She insisted on washing the feet of forty-one old and poor women—she was herself now forty-one—afterwards going six times round the hall in which they sat, giving them, on successive journeys, food and wine, cloth "of royal weave," shoes and stockings, purses containing forty-one pennies, aprons and towels. At the end, she gave to the oldest and poorest woman, the rich, furred, purple gown which she had worn for the ceremony. And as the choristers chanted the *Miserere* and other psalms, reciting at each verse: "In those days there was, in the city, a woman who was a sinner," she found the words matching the reiterated monotony of her thoughts: Was it her sinfulness that caused all she intended for good to turn to evil, that brought danger where she sought safety, hate where she purposed love, heresy where she strove for the Faith?

The only concession she made to safety was when, next

day, Good Friday, she "touched" for "King's Evil." Her council realized that, at this traditional ceremony, potential murderers could easily present themselves among the scrofulous seeking healing, and eventually managed to prevail on her to perform the act privately in a gallery where only her guards and twenty people of known loyalty were present, while the sick were admitted one by one. By her side stood Pole, priest and Primate, who gave her absolution before she started to lay hands on the sick.

If one only had been healed, she would have taken heart. But she was given no sign, though in her dereliction she gave it to others. The Venetian Ambassador was constrained to break off his political and diplomatic reporting of his next letter to the Doge to record: "Her Majesty struck me as affording a great and rare example of goodness, performing all those acts with such humility and love, offering up her prayers to God with so great devotion and affection and enduring for so long a while and so patiently so much fatigue that I dare assert that there was never a Queen in Christendom of greater goodness than this one, whom I pray God long to save and prosper."

So they came to Easter. In that promise of renewal, she steeled herself to make one last effort to set things to rights. On Easter Monday, she wrote to Charles.

"My Lord and good Father," the letter ran, humbly exposing her vulnerable honesty, "I thank you humbly for remembering me where the return of the King, my husband, is concerned, as I have seen from your letters and messages. Now that the abdication is over, I implore Your Majesty most humbly, for the love of God, to do all that is possible to permit it. I beg Your Majesty to forgive my boldness and to remember the unspeakable sadness I experience because of the absence of the King, which emboldens me thus to write to you, who have always shown me a more than paternal affection."

In the Tower, Throgmorton, under examination, denied that he had said that Mary had taken Philip's portrait and kicked it out of the Privy Chamber. And at Wimbledon, Cecil was careful to go first of all with the parishioners to make his Easter confession and receive Communion. He gave an edifying example of piety in saying his rosary and, since no one knew what these difficult times might bring forth, he took away with him the Parish Register so that, if the worst came to the worst, he could produce documentary proof of his Catholic fervor.

Elizabeth, at Hatfield, started to draft an elaborate letter of condolence to Mary that such enormities as conspiracies should exist: "When I revolve in mind, most noble Queen, the old love of paynims for their princes and the reverent fear of Romans to their Senate, I cannot but muse for my part, and blush for theirs, to see the rebellious hearts and devilish intents of Christians in name but Jews in deed, toward their anointed King, which methinks, if they had feared God (though they could not have loved the state), they should, for the dread of their own plague, have refrained that wickedness . . ."

On second thoughts, however, she decided that complete silence was the safer until it was quite clear how much had been discovered.

## SIXTEEN

# A
# *Matter of*
# *Conscience*

Too much was discovered. Under torture or the threat of it, all the prisoners except Throgmorton confessed what they knew. More than one implicated Elizabeth and revealed the state of affairs at Hatfield. Consequently, at the beginning of June, Kate Ashley, Battista Castiglione and three of the domestic staff were arrested, and Elizabeth was left to face a month of suspense with what equanimity she could muster. But she was in less danger than she feared. Mary had always accepted the fact that, innocent or guilty, she was bound to be at the center of every plot. Now she had, in addition, schooled herself to admit that, as an issue of practical politics, it hardly mattered whether or not she was there by her own will and consent. Though Mary assumed her sister's willing participation, the treachery was negligible compared with the possibility of a French invasion and the discovery that Lord Thomas Howard, Lord Braye, Lord Delaware, and a dozen of the minor nobility, including Cecil's brother-in-law, were active traitors.

Consequently, after the arrest of two more gentlemen of Elizabeth's household, the Queen decided that, after all, she might as well play this hand of the game according to the Princess's rules. She sent the Master of Horse and a Privy Councilor down to Hatfield to comfort and console her. They assured Elizabeth of Mary's goodwill. They explained that the Queen understood perfectly how dejected and distressed she must be at the discovery that, unwittingly, she had traitors among her servants. They recited, in detail, the substance of their confessions, implicating her. Then they presented her with a valuable ring as a token of Mary's love and esteem and hoped that her unhappy experience would in the end be profitable by revealing the dangers of a too great trust in unworthy servants into which she had been led by her youth and inexperience.

Elizabeth was terrified and wondered if, after all, she had been underestimating Mary's intelligence.

She composed a letter with even more care than usual. "Among earthly things," she wrote, "I chiefly wish this one—that there were as good surgeons for making anatomies of hearts (that I might show my thoughts to Your Majesty), as there are expert physicians of bodies, able to express the inward griefs of maladies to their patients. For then I doubt not, but know well, that whatever others should suggest by malice, yet Your Majesty should be sure, by knowledge, that the more such mists render effuscate the clear light of my soul, the more my tried thoughts should lighten by the dimming of their hidden malice. But since wishes are vain and desires oft fail, I must crave that my deeds may supply that which my thoughts cannot declare, and that they be not mis-deemed, as the facts have been so well tried. And like as I have been your faithful subject from the beginning of your reign, so shall no wicked person cause me to change to the end of my life." She subscribed herself: "Your Majesty's obedient subject and humble sister."

But Mary was too weary, too ill and too occupied with other matters to pay much attention either to her style or to her protests.

Summer, as if to atone for the continuous rain of its predecessor, had this year provided a more intense heat and a more prolonged drought than anyone could remember; yet in spite of the discomfort, the Queen insisted on staying in London until the trials and executions of the leading conspirators were over. She felt she must remain at the center of affairs until she set out to meet Philip at Dover. This time he would not disappoint her. He would certainly arrive before July 25, to celebrate with her their wedding-day. On July 14, however, she received a letter from him saying that the arrival in Brussels of his brother-in-law and sister, the King and Queen of Bohemia, gave rise to new discussions for which his father demanded his continuing presence there. Though he could no longer bind himself to any stated time, he would, of course, return as soon as practicable. In the meantime, would Mary send an official representative to welcome the visitors? Charles, also, wrote requesting this diplomatic courtesy.

Mary's control at last snapped. After an outburst of rage in which Pole almost feared for her reason, she wrote not to Philip but to Charles. Her hand was still trembling and she made no attempt to disguise her feelings, even omitting her invariable "Good Father," as she wrote

151

formally: "My Lord: Now that June is over and July drawing to an end, it would be pleasanter for me to be able to thank Your Majesty for sending me back the King, my lord and good husband, than to despatch an emissary to Flanders to visit my good brother the King of Bohemia and the Queen his wife. However, as Your Majesty has been pleased to break your promise in this connection, a promise you made to me concerning the return of the King, my husband, I must perforce be satisfied although to my unspeakable regret." Then, at last, emaciated, unable to sleep and indifferent to death, she consented to leave London and retire to her palace at Eltham.

But Philip was relentless. Instead of remembrances for the anniversary of their own marriage came more peremptory demands for her consent to Elizabeth's marriage to Savoy. What right had she to continue to oppose it? She had better examine her conscience with care, since her refusal was not only further endangering peace in England and playing into the hands of the French King, but was impeding the consolidation of the Faith in Europe. When Charles in the near future returned to Spain, he might call at Dover to take Elizabeth with him to present her to Savoy.

This time, Mary's anger was colder and her reply longer considered. She drafted it carefully, altering it here and there—"most humbly beg" instead of "ask"—so that the softening of the tone should disguise the asperity of the content: "I will say nothing now except that seeing you hold that I should examine my conscience to know if it is in conformity with the truth or no, to beg Your Highness most humbly to name and appoint what persons you judge fit to speak with me about this affair, *for the thing my conscience holds, it has held for this four and twenty*

152

*years*. I beseech you in all humility to put off this business till your return, and then you shall judge if I am blame-worthy or no. To be plain with you, according to my simple judgment and under Your Highness's correction, seeing that the Duke of Savoy is just now away at the war and certain of the Council and nobility of this realm with Your Highness, I cannot see in what way the affair could be well managed, nor to my mind (even if my conscience were as clear about it as yours) could it come to the end you desire without your presence here. Wherefore, my lord, in as humble sort as I may, I, your most true and obedient wife, beg Your Majesty that we two should pray to God that we may live and come together again; and that very God, Who has the thoughts of the hearts of princes in His hand, will, I make no doubt, so enlighten us that the outcome shall be to His glory and your content."

Would Philip at least understand that, until they were together again as man and wife, nothing could be decided even about Elizabeth? What her conscience held could remain a secret for ever if only they had a child to succeed them. The false pregnancy did not preclude a true pregnancy. Of that she was certain. But as long as the world knew they were apart, so long would men turn to her sister as her heir.

Hardly had she dispatched the letter than one more proof came of the danger. A fleet of Protestants-turned-pirate and financed by the King of France put ashore another pretender on the coast of Sussex, who asserted that he was Courtenay come to marry Elizabeth. Before he was arrested, the people in the neighborhood proclaimed Elizabeth Queen. But at Eltham, Mary could struggle no more. The fleet was left to deal with the pirates and the

Lords of the Council with the pretender. The Queen received the news of the capture of the one and the hanging of the other as one in a dream.

She had sunk into such a lassitude of melancholy that Pole, alarmed, arranged for her to leave Eltham and go to his own residence, the palace of the Archbishops of Canterbury at Croydon. Here, deep in the country, with him by her side, she slowly recovered her hold on life and for a few brief weeks, savored the joy of not being Queen. Her greatest pleasure was in walking, plainly dressed, with her ladies and visiting the cottages of the poor, relieving their wants, playing with their children. They did not even know who she was, but they grew to love the short-sighted, deep-voiced "lady from the palace" with her bustling walk and matter-of-fact ways, who had obviously come to regain her health after an illness. Indoors, she worked on the great tapestry of the Garden of Eden which her mother and Pole's had started but had had no time to finish. In the hidden peace of that high summer, the plants and the birds and the beasts of the English countryside found their way into the paradise of innocence to give a tired woman some momentary respite from a too-fallen world.

Then, one September evening when she was walking with Pole on a lawn bordered by the trees which, among all things in nature, were to him the most lovely, he told her that he had received an intimation that the Emperor was on the point of setting out for Spain. A return to London would be necessary.

"You feel strong enough now, Mary, to take up the burden again?"

She nodded.

"But first, Reynald, I must have your judgment on a matter of conscience."

"What is troubling you?"

"It is still Elizabeth's marriage."

"That is hardly a matter of conscience; and we have discussed it often enough. Leave it till Philip returns."

"You agree with Philip, Reynald."

"I have never committed myself."

"But you do," she persisted.

"I admit I see nothing against it. To have your sister out of England now would strengthen us here. To have her Duchess of Savoy would strengthen the position abroad. But how can your conscience be concerned in it? You are only obeying your husband, as is your duty. If there is any blame for it, it is on his conscience, not yours."

Mary hesitated, fumbling for a phrasing of her question. "But how if by my silence I have deceived you all?"

"How can that be?"

"Elizabeth is a bastard."

"In law, yes. Since Anne Boleyn was not your father's true wife, no one disputes that. But it may be politic to cease to insist too much on it. She can be legitimated."

Pole spoke almost impatiently. This argument had proceeded for years; it was not, at this moment, of practical importance.

"I do not mean that at all," said Mary. "I mean that Elizabeth is not my sister. She is not my father's daughter."

"Then who——"

"Her father was Mark Smeaton, Anne Boleyn's dancing-man."

For a moment Pole thought the Queen must again be ill and fallen a prey to sick fancies, but he was soon undeceived. She was as calm and as matter-of-fact as if she had

155

been at a meeting of the Council discussing an economic measure and he knew her well enough to be certain that she was not attempting to deceive him, even though she herself might have been deceived. Besides, the matter was not, of itself, improbable. Everyone knew that Mark Smeaton had been Anne Boleyn's lover. Twenty years ago, the young man had died the terrible death for high treason, glorying in it. The child of whom Anne had miscarried when Elizabeth was three was his—Pole had heard of that in Italy, where it was the gossip of diplomacy—so that it was at least possible that Elizabeth had the same paternity.

Pole, dredging his memory, managed to call up, faintly at first but growing clearer, the image of the tall, elegant dancer and musician who had been much in evidence at Court in the years immediately before his exile. So when Mary said: "Think, Reynald! Is not Elizabeth so like him that it is a wonder everyone does not see it?" he was able to answer: "When I meet Elizabeth face to face, I shall know better; but it seems to me, now you have said it, that there is a likeness. But you have more proof than that?"

"At Elizabeth's christening, the ladies all said it was so, especially old Margaret. They jested about it. No one troubled to hide it from me. I was there, you know, and seventeen."

"Who else?"

"I am not sure. None living now. I think Thomas More knew. And Gardiner. He'd have got rid of Elizabeth, if he could. And my father faced it at the end. He sent for me when he knew he was dying and asked me to be a mother to Edward. But there was no word for Elizabeth. He hated her and would not see her."

"Have you told Philip?"

"No. I have told no one but you; and I am telling you as my confessor and under the seal. Even that is only because to judge, you must first know. As I see it, I must do nothing which can be construed as an acknowledgement that Elizabeth is of royal blood."

"But you have always treated her as a sister."

"And will, as far as she will let me, in the ordinary way of living. But not in State matters. That, in conscience, I cannot do. I am right, Reynald, am I not? Bess is only Mark Smeaton's child and not for any throne."

They talked over the events of twenty years ago, he testing her knowledge here, supplementing it there. In the gathering dusk of the quiet garden, Mark might have been present, an ironic, elegant ghost recalled by the intensity of remembrance.

Smeaton had been the son of poor parents who, by his grace in dancing and his skill in music, had early won a place at Court. When Anne Boleyn became the King's *maîtresse-en-titre*, he joined her household. She first became personally aware of him one morning at Winchester when, lying in bed in her rooms above the King's, she sent for a musician to play so that her ladies could dance. Smeaton was chosen and as Anne watched him she set her heart on having him for a lover. He was her own age —twenty-three—and Henry was an elderly forty. As, either through indifference or fear, he would take no advantage of her obvious interest, she took into her confidence her old and trusted waiting-woman, Margaret, who at night lay in the ante-chamber to her room between it and the gallery where the rest of her ladies slept. In this ante-chamber was a cupboard where sweetmeats, candied fruits and preserves were kept.

Here, one night, Margaret concealed Smeaton. When all was quiet and the ladies-in-waiting in bed, Anne called out, loudly enough for them to hear: "Margaret, bring me a little marmalade," and the waiting-woman, leading Smeaton by the hand, said: "Here is the marmalade, my lady." Then Anne, for the benefit of the ladies in the gallery, called out: "Go along: go to bed," and the lovers were left together.

The love-affair, which started two years before the birth of Elizabeth, continued for five years when they both went to death for it. Its intensity, on Smeaton's part at least, never waned. But he grew careless. He spent Anne's liberal gifts to him on dress and jewels and horses. He became overbearing and insolent, after the traditional manner of lowborn favorites, and quarreled with some of the courtiers, in particular with the brother of the Earl of Northumberland, Sir Thomas Percy.

Anne, when she heard of this, was alarmed. She sent for Percy and ordered him to make up his quarrel with Mark. Though forced to obey, he harbored a sufficient grudge to go to the all-powerful Secretary of State, Thomas Cromwell, tell him of the favor the Queen was showing to her musician and to point out that Smeaton could not have got by fair means the money he was in the habit of ostentatiously spending.

The information arrived at a time when, for political reasons, Anne was in deadly danger. Henry, his early passion swiftly spent, had long tired of her and was openly in love with Jane Seymour. Catherine of Aragon had died that winter, and as Cranmer was ready, at Henry's bidding, to proclaim the marriage with Anne (which he had celebrated) null and void, there was now nothing to prevent him marrying Jane. He had, indeed, told Anne with

158

brutal directness that, unless she gave him a son, he would rid himself of her. Her desperation had increased since, as justice would have it, she miscarried of a son on the day of Catherine of Aragon's funeral.

Cromwell, anxious to please the King by ridding him of Anne, was delighted at Percy's information. Every movement of Mark Smeaton was watched and the musician became frightened by the crushing atmosphere of menace. Though no politician, he realized that he was at the center of a struggle for power between Cromwell and the Boleyn faction, led by Anne's brave and brilliant brother, George. There was too much at stake for him to dare to remain at Court and he decided to leave it until things had blown over. On May Eve, he took his farewell of Anne, warning her also. He left her apartments at Greenwich early in the morning, but before he could arrive in London, he was arrested and tortured into a confession.

The rest of the proceedings were public enough. Into the net were brought four of the ablest of Anne's supporters including her brother George, all of whom were accused of adultery with her. All the charges were denied and unproved; that of incest was laughable and George Boleyn defended himself at his trial with such cogency, passion and eloquence that the betting in the city was ten to one that he would be acquitted. But he was reckless enough in open court to repeat his charge, based on certain knowledge, that Henry was impotent and that Elizabeth was not his child; and he was condemned and died with the rest.

But Mark Smeaton was in a different category. It was not only that he was reckoned a menial, merely, and so was denied the quick death of the others, but had to suffer castration and disemboweling before he was allowed to

159

die. It was that, from first to last, he refused to deny his love. He immediately pleaded guilty and never retracted it. On the scaffold, he reasserted it and so went to his end . . .

As Mary spoke of these events which, though twenty years had passed, seemed but yesterday, she made them more vivid for Pole by remembering her own part in them. There was the visit to her of the Emperor Charles's ambassador to tell her that Henry's intention to bastardize Elizabeth by admitting Smeaton's paternity had been suddenly prevented by George Boleyn's public statement of his impotence. There was Henry's message to her by her half-brother, Richmond—the King's eldest illegitimate son: "You should thank God for escaping that cursed and venomous whore who tried to poison you both," which she did not altogether believe, though she knew well enough how Anne had hated her and wished her dead. There was, above all, her triumphant return to her father's side, after her long exile from Court, when Henry, who had for years refused to see her, gave her once more his affection and confidence. It was then at the very center of things that she had made certain of the truth of Elizabeth's parentage. By the quirk of obstinacy in her nature, she became at that moment the child's champion, and though bidden, in common with all the Court, never to use the title of "Princess" for her, she insisted, despite Henry's anger, on referring to her as "Her Grace."

And the private courtesy she had paid to a helpless child she continued to pay, and would, to the grown woman who, inheriting her mother's ambition and courage and her father's charm and grace, had designs on her life and her throne. What she would not do was to take any step which, implicitly or explicitly, would recognize Elizabeth

Philip II of Spain, the Tardy Bridegroom, found "that Mary was indeed Henry's daughter ..."

Cardinal Pole . . .
"shared her troubles
. . . prayed for
her soul. . . ."

Archbishop Cranmer
. . . "would die like
Samson, pulling down
the house on
his enemies."

as her heir. That would outrage her family, her throne and her country. Was she right?

Pole, whose diplomatic mind did not see the problems so simply, merely said: "You have said that it is a matter of conscience and that, as you know, is the ultimate sanction. But you must tell Philip when he returns. And you have Elizabeth on your side."

"How? She does not know. Nor would she believe it if she were told."

"I mean in the matter of marriage. She has no wish to marry Savoy. You are at one there."

Mary was delighted. It was an aspect of the problem she had overlooked. Now, on one matter at least, she and Bess could stand unequivocally together. It would be a combination that no one could break.

"I will send for her to Court," she said, "when we return to London. Thank you, Reynald."

# SEVENTEEN

# The Return of the King

W HEN, IN the autumn, Elizabeth received Mary's invitation to Court, she was at a loss to assess its significance. It was prefaced by the release from prison of Kate Ashley and Battista Castiglione, with no punishment other than being forbidden ever to return to her household, and by the removal of Sir Thomas Pope from his post as her comptroller. This was clemency, of a sort; but Elizabeth, during the uncertain months, had become increasingly certain that Mary was under no illusions as to what had actually happened. She attributed her own reinstatement less to her sister's trust than to the change in the political situation, which had given Mary a new confidence. Among other indications of this were Pole's freeing of all the Protestants confined at Lambeth on their mere promise "to keep themselves good and true to God and to the King and Queen," and the release of Cecil's in-

triguing brother-in-law after a long interview with the
Cardinal, in which he affected to embrace Catholicism.

Overshadowing everything as far as Elizabeth's own
position was concerned was Courtenay's death in Italy
which had removed a potential monarch from the
checker-board of politics. No longer could "an English
King and Queen" be the proclaimed object of rebellion
and, to that extent, Elizabeth realized that her status was
diminished. She knew, too, that de Noailles's recall to
France and his replacement as Ambassador by his softer
and less perceptive brother had further weakened the con-
spiratorial side in England, while the uneasy truce between
the warring nations abroad, even if it had made no practical difference to the French King's encouragement, had
forced him theoretically to discontinue it.

Fortunately for her peace of mind, she did not know—
what Mary knew—that he had come to the conclusion
that, since the legitimate heir to the English crown, the fif-
teen-year-old Mary Queen of Scots, was about to marry
the Dauphin, his best policy was not merely to abandon
Elizabeth but to ask the Pope publicly to declare her a
bastard so that there could be no question of her standing
in the way of his daughter-in-law's eventual occupancy of
the English throne. She was, indeed, surprised that, when
she sent her emissary, the Countess of Sussex, heavily disguised, to ask the new French Ambassador for instructions, she was merely told to do nothing; but she attributed
the required quiesence to the truce. Her complacency
was further fortified by observing that, ironically, Mary's
consolidation of a Catholic England was now being imperiled by the private nationalist obsessions of the octo-
genarian Pope, who in his intense hatred of all things

Spanish was preparing, in alliance with France, an attack on Philip through his kingdom of Naples.

Mary, on her side had, throughout the autumn, realized that for the first time in her reign, Elizabeth had ceased to be a menace to her. France was preparing another attack, but now, because Courtenay was dead and the French King's policy had changed, it was no longer through Bess. Her Ambassador in Paris had informed her of the intended blow, though he was unable to give complete information. All he could say was that "neither Dudley nor any of the English gentlemen in France were privy to the matter." This, of itself, exonerated Elizabeth.

So when Elizabeth entered London on a bright November day to take up her residence at Somerset House, she was free to enjoy the welcome of the Londoners. It could no longer excite Mary's jealousy. As, accompanied by her red-coated gentlemen, she came riding through Smithfield, past the Old Bailey and up Fleet Street to the Strand, she acknowledged the people's cheers without fear and savored something of the sweetness of what she was certain would come when Dr. Dee's horoscope should be at last fulfilled.

Her meeting with Mary next day at St. James's was even more satisfactory. As they kissed each other it seemed for the moment as if one of their brief childhood alliances, when Mary was protective and Elizabeth grateful, had survived into the present. Elizabeth found herself genuinely shocked to see how Mary had aged since their last meeting and how sad and ill she looked.

The Queen came straight to the point: "Elizabeth, I have heard once more from the King that he is determined on your marriage to his cousin of Savoy."

Elizabeth parried with: "And is it your wish also?"

"I can have no wishes of my own," said Mary. "It is for me to try to do what is right and just. A woman's duty is to her husband, a Queen's to her people. Your choice, Bess, is the simpler."

"As a loyal subject, I have no choice apart from yours."

"I give it you."

"Then I may say it. I do not wish to marry Savoy. I wish to marry no one. If I could have my own way I would live and die a virgin."

"In one thing at least you shall have your own way," said Mary. "If you refuse Savoy, I will stand by you in your refusal."

"But if the King insists?"

"By law and custom and my father's will, I could not have married without the consent of my Council. Neither can you marry Savoy. When the Lords of the Council know that both you and I are against it, they will, I have no doubt, act as they should. You need fear nothing. The Cardinal, too, will reassure you."

Next day, Elizabeth, at Mary's request, went to Lambeth to consult Pole on the matter. Though she had feared this first meeting with the man who had been so bitter an enemy of her mother and whose house had been destroyed because of it, his regal kindliness put her immediately at her ease. And, on the matter of the Savoy marriage, she found him as definite as Mary had been. On his side, as soon as she entered the room, the face and hands of Mark Smeaton became clear in his memory. But he was sorry that it was so. He thought she had much charm and a great spirit, and would have made an admirable Duchess of Savoy.

At that moment, however, he was too burdened by the complexities of the international situation to see either her marriage or Mary's conscientious objection to it as anything but the slightest of problems. Compared with the impending scandal of a war between Philip and the Pope, into which England might be dragged, they were but as a mote to a beam. His own position, as Philip's *de facto* Regent and the Pope's *de jure* Legate, while it made him the obvious mediator also exposed him to a double accusation of disloyalty. Never, in his long experience of diplomacy, had he encountered such a situation. He wrote to both of them. To Philip he offered to cross the Channel, should the promised return be longer delayed, so that he might by word of mouth reinforce his arguments for peace. To the Pope, he adopted a different tone and dared to remind him: "When Satan demanded the sons of the Church that he might sift them like wheat, Christ resisted with the sole remedy of prayer and commanded us to use this same remedy. This is what we hope will come to pass so much the more easily because those things which estranged the minds of Your Holiness and the King arose not from yourselves but from your ministers and seem to me so recent that they cannot have taken deep root in your minds in so short a time."

The only effect on His Holiness was to make him revoke Pole's Legateship and order him to return to Rome to stand his trial for suspected heresy, on account of his leniency to English Protestants. But the King decided at last to terminate his nearly-two-years' absence and go back to England, if for no other reason than to persuade Mary to declare war on France. In his train, Philip would bring his cousin, the Duchess of Lorraine, who could take Elizabeth back with her for her marriage with Savoy.

On a March day, his courier arrived at Greenwich to announce that he had set out for Calais where he would embark at the first favorable wind. The emissary Philip had chosen for this good news was that magnificent young man of twenty-five, Lord Robert Dudley, who, for proclaiming his sister-in-law Lady Jane Grey Queen, had been sent to the Tower at the same time as Elizabeth but had been released, at Philip's request, to accompany him to Flanders. As he now entered the Presence Chamber to make his welcome announcement, he glanced quickly at Elizabeth, sitting at Mary's side and as their eyes met and for a second held each other's she knew that her world was changed.

She and Robin had known each other from childhood. Roger Ascham, the Cambridge scholar who later became secretary to Elizabeth the Queen, had taught them both, commending her Latin at the expense of his. Always she had liked him, but when, at the nadir of her fortunes in the Tower, he had contrived to bribe the warder so that he could visit her and give her comfort, the accepted friendship deepened with gratitude. The turmoil and terror of that time had, however, made for a disturbed judgment and her head, weighing matters of mere safety, had protected her heart. She had not seen him again and now all her defenses went down before his sudden, unexpected entry.

The wars had given an assurance to his elegance. The superb body, the clear-cut features, the commanding head, the shapely expressive hands had gained maturity. Here was a man. Here, she now knew beyond power of any dissuasion, was her man. That he had a wife was of no consequence. Amy Robsart could be dealt with when the time came. Robin must be hers and hers only. And, for her part, if she could not have him, she would have no one. She would, as she had told Mary she wished to, live and die a virgin. But now that conventional protestation assumed the terrible urgency of truth. And Mary, who would protect her against Emmanuel Philibert, became a guardian angel. As she watched how her sister, listening to Robin's description of Philip, became almost young again and how life and passion returned to the listless, tired eyes, Elizabeth was drawn to her as she would never have believed possible. What were they both, after all, but two women in love, sick for their men? She found herself approving Mary's quick order that a ship was to lie immediately in Calais roads, ready in everything, "so that, at his arrival there, His Majesty would not be forced to stay one hour longer than he need."

Three days later, Philip arrived at Greenwich. It was five in the afternoon when, in the March twilight, he stepped ashore at the water-gate to a salute of sixteen guns from the ship which had brought him and the crew's shouts of "God save the King and Queen." At the first sight of him, Mary surrendered utterly. The doubts and the anger and the frustrations of absence vanished as if they had never been. It was enough that he was home and she was his even more completely than at that first meeting in Winchester.

Next day, which was Sunday, they proceeded in state through the royal gallery to their private chapel, to hear Mass, while, in every church in London, the *Te Deum* was sung. But Pole was not there. As soon as Philip's return was announced, he had asked Mary's permission to retire to Canterbury, free at last to attend to his spiritual duties in his see. And for those first days, Mary did not even miss him.

She decided that there must be some outward and visible symbol to mark the inauguration of this new order of hope

in England. Already she had restored Westminster Abbey
to the Benedictines from whom her father had taken it for
plunder. But one thing was still unrestored. The shrine of
St. Edward the Confessor, at the very heart of it, was still
in disrepair and his relics still lay in the hole into which
they had been hurried when the triumphant Protestants
had looted and desecrated the shrine. Mary now ordered
that they should be reinterred with great ceremony in a
shrine as perfectly restored as possible. It was to be ready
for St. George's Day, so that the celebration should honor
the two patron saints of England and, at a Pontifical High
Mass, attended by all the Knights of the Garter with the
King at their head, the spiritual and the temporal should
be drawn together in an act of unforgettable splendor.

And so it was done. One thing only was lacking. She
herself, once more overtaken by sickness, was too ill to be
there.

# EIGHTEEN

# *War*

T<small>HAT WEEK</small> the French struck. Their new instrument was revealed as young Thomas Stafford, scion of that semi-royal house of Buckingham which, posing as a champion of the people, had for a century menaced the Crown. Thomas's great-grandfather, the second Duke, had intrigued against and been executed by Richard III. His grandfather, the third Duke, had intrigued against and been executed by Henry VIII. His father, Lord Stafford, learning thus by example the wisdom of accommodation, had assumed a somewhat conventional fidelity to whomever happened to be on the throne, while his mother, Cardinal Pole's sister, was, like all her house genuinely devoted to Mary. But in him, their second son, all the inheritance of family ambition and intrigue seemed to have concentrated itself, and as he was of Plantagenet blood on both sides he was admirably fitted to the French King's purpose.

He had already caused his uncle sufficient embarrassment. When Pole had been in France in the spring of that year whose summer was to see Mary's marriage to Philip and autumn his own return to England as Legate, Thomas Stafford had suddenly called on the Cardinal at Fontainebleau. He explained that he, with several of his friends, had left England on account of the proposed Spanish match and implored Pole to use his influence against it. The fact that the Cardinal, on hearing this, had, in a towering rage, ordered him to leave his presence and never enter it again had not prevented the French court buzzing with rumors, started by Stafford, that Pole had agreed with him and intended to take the title of Duke of York and offer himself to Mary as an alternative bridegroom to Philip.

And now, three years after, Stafford decided that he himself might be England's deliverer from the Spanish tyranny. The King of France provided 3,000 troops for Scotland to attack Berwick at the appropriate time and, on the voyage, one of the ships, the *Fleur de Lys*, put Stafford ashore with a small force at Scarborough, whose ill-guarded castle he easily surprised. He issued a proclamation as "Protector and Governor of the Realm" in which he alleged that twelve English castles were about to be handed over to the Spaniards, so that they could keep England in subjection. He explained that Spaniards, including the half-Spanish Mary, would rather live with "Turks, Jews and Moors" than with the English whom they intended to treat with great cruelty. In consequence, he, of that house of Buckingham which had always stood with the Commons against tyrants, had come to save England from this "devilish device of Mary, unrightful and unworthy Queen of England, who, by the laws of this noble realm of England hath forfeit the Crown for a marriage with a stranger."

Had his appearance been in Kent or Essex, where treason and propaganda were well organized, he might have had some success. But in loyal Yorkshire the seed of rebellion fell on notably stony ground. Not a man joined him. The local militia, without bloodshed, recaptured Scarborough Castle and hanged him, with twenty-seven of his men, as a warning to any other potential "Protectors" and "Governors."

Yet the final effect of the fool's errand was out of all proportion to its importance. For one thing, it drove Mary and Elizabeth still closer together, for not only did it demonstrate to Mary Elizabeth's innocence in this particular plot, but it showed Elizabeth, beyond possibility of mistake, that the new pattern of French policy was directed against her as much as against Mary.

The main beneficiary was Philip. During his five weeks in England he had realized that his hope of English support in his war with France was illusory. The temper of the Council, as well as of the country, was set on enforcing that clause of his marriage contract which provided that England should not be expected to take part in any of Spain's wars. But now that it seemed that the French might attempt an invasion and beacons had to be kept ready along the coasts, the whole atmosphere changed. Moreover, England's safety was bound up with that of the Low Countries and her age-old policy was to go to war with any invader of Flanders. To repel the French on those fields was mere self-interest. Though it would mean fighting side-by-side with Spaniards as allies, it could not be construed as a war on behalf of Spain. Consequently, the Council, reflecting the temper of the country no less than Philip's desires, voted for war, and throughout May military preparations proceeded energetically.

Early in June, "according to the magnanimous custom of this realm never to go to war without first giving notice," Norroy, King of Arms, presented himself at the court of France, while in London, on the same day, a proclamation was made that England and France were at war.

In it, Mary summarized the disquiet of her short reign: "Although we, the Queen, when we first came to the throne, understood that the Duke of Northumberland's abominable treason had been abetted by the French King and that since then his ministers had secretly favoured Wyatt's rebellion, such was our care for the peace of Christendom and the repose of our subjects, that we attributed these doings to the French King's ministers rather than to his own will. Lately, when Dudley and Ashton started a new conspiracy, the King's ambassador was not only cognizant of it but received them in his house and supported them in their diabolical undertaking. He has also favoured pirates, enemies of Christendom, who have despoiled our subjects. We realize that nothing we can do will induce the King to change his methods. The other day he sent Stafford with ships and supplies to seize our castle of Scarborough, not content with having intrigued so long with a view to getting possession of Calais and other places belonging to us across the seas, and having financed counterfeiters and encouraged them to put false coin into circulation in this country. For the above reasons and because he has sent an army to invade Flanders which we are under obligation to defend, we have seen fit to proclaim to our subjects that they are to consider the King of France as a public enemy to ourselves and our nation."

In Rheims, as the herald started to read the declaration, Henri II interrupted him with: "Who sent you?"

"The Queen of England, my mistress."

"Where is the patent?"

Norroy handed it to the King and again tried to read what he had to say. But Henri had no wish for the ambassadors of other nations to hear the extent of his encouragement of English treason set out in so plain a manner. Again he interrupted: "I forbid you, on your life, to speak another word."

Norroy, about to protest, was silenced by: "I am acting thus because you come in the name of a woman. Were England ruled by a King, I would listen. But you may tell her this. I have always observed towards her good faith and amity. Now that she picks so unjust a quarrel with me, I hope that God will be pleased to grant me this grace —that she shall gain no more by it than her predecessors did when they attacked mine. You will now depart and leave my kingdom as quickly as you can."

Norroy, reporting the interview, found Mary oddly undisturbed by the insult. Whatever weaknesses the woman might have, lack of a warlike courage was not one of them. As she had twice put herself at the head of her subjects to crush rebellion, so she would again, if necessary, to wage war. The French in Flanders were Philip's affair; but, she told him, if they attacked through Scotland, as it was supposed they would, she herself, in his absence, would ride north to lead her army against them.

Yet during the hot June days that followed the break with France, what she most needed was courage of a different order. Philip was impatient to be gone, for he had determined to conduct the war in person, with Savoy as his second-in-command. Her days with him were numbered and she had a sick presentiment that this time he would not come back. Wanting him with her every relentless moment of the short interim, she yet forced herself to let him go—to enjoy hunting expeditions where she

175

could not accompany him; to conduct warlike consultations from which she was excluded. She felt she had less claim on him now that her own obsessing matter had been decided. He had understood and approved her objection to Elizabeth's marriage when she had explained it to him and the Duchess of Lorraine, after a mere month's stay, had left England without either the Princess or an invitation to return.

On Midsummer Day, Mary gave a great party for Philip to which Elizabeth was invited in state, so that all the world might know the amity which was now between them. Early in the morning, she sent to Somerset House her own Royal barge, festooned with garlands of flowers and covered with an awning of green silk, embroidered with honeysuckle and marigolds. Under the canopy Elizabeth sat in state, attended by Sir Thomas Pope, who had been restored as Comptroller of her Household, and four of her ladies-of-honor. There followed in six boats Elizabeth's gentlemen dressed in russet damask and blue satin, with caps of silver cloth and green plumes.

Philip and Mary received her in the gardens of Richmond Palace, where a sumptuous entertainment had been prepared in a pavilion specially constructed in the labyrinth in the form of a castle made of cloth of gold and purple velvet, embroidered with silver fleur-de-lis and Catherine of Aragon's device of the pomegranate in gold. After the banquet was a concert, in which the best musicians in England performed, before Elizabeth returned to London in the same manner as she had come.

A week later, Philip went hunting in English woods for the last time and on July 3 he and Mary set out slowly and with magnificence for the coast. Not again would she part with him at Greenwich but would come with him to the edge of Kentish soil. At Sittingbourne they slept the first night, at Canterbury the second. On the third, at Dover, they did not sleep. Wind and tide dictated time and at three in the morning of July 6, the Octave Day of St. Peter and St. Paul, he left her, dry-eyed, on the strand and went aboard for France.

## NINETEEN

# "Calais Written on My Heart"

THE STAKE was Calais—"the principal member and chief jewel of our realm," as Mary described it. Of this, no one was in any doubt. Wherever the war might reach, however the tides of it might ebb and flow, Calais was for France the ultimate prize and for England the not-to-be-thought-of loss. This hundred and twenty square miles of England-in-France, the last remnant of Edward III's conquests, with its roads and canals to serve and forts to defend the city-port, had for two centuries been England's doorway to the Continent and, with Dover, the twin-guardian of the Narrow Seas. It had become over the years veritably English, even in the names—Coquelle was now Calkwall; Wissant, Whitsand—and it returned two Members to the English House of Commons.

In charge of it was the thirty-three-year-old Lord Wentworth who, though an enthusiastic Protestant, had shown his loyalty to Mary in the first rebellion of her reign and had taken the field for her against Northumberland. She herself did not doubt his continuing fidelity, though she had not been able to forget Gardiner's shrewd warning, not long before he died, that Calais was so full of heretics that, if Wentworth were not removed, Calais would not be English for more than a year longer. If she minimized the danger of treachery, it was, partly at least, because she could not bring herself to believe that hatred of her Faith would go to such lengths. She was more concerned with the strength of the defenses and the numbers of the garrison, though she did not know that the French Ambassador, on his way home after the declaration of war, had managed to make a careful study of the one and that Sir Henry Dudley kept the French informed of the other; and that both recommended a surprise attack as certain to succeed.

The opening stages of the war, however, lay nearer France's heart. The garrison at St. Quentin blocked the road from Flanders to Paris. The Duke of Savoy was besieging it and, soon after the English force joined him, the French's great relieving force of 24,000 men and twenty pieces of artillery came up and battle was joined. Savoy gained a total victory on August 10—the feast day of St. Laurence, to whom Philip had a special devotion. As thanksgiving, the King vowed to build a great monastery dedicated to the saint at El Escorial, a little village not far from Madrid, while in England the Queen ordered *Te Deums* to be sung and processions to be made. When, a fortnight later, St. Quentin fell, England greeted the news with bonfires of rejoicing and, as it was reported that the English were in the forefront of the enterprise, a blaze of victorious patriotism welded the divided country, for a few brief weeks, into one. Further victories and—even more welcome—the conclusion of peace between Philip and the Pope called for further festivities and, as autumn became winter, the triumph of England was regarded as certain.

Yet, though the way to Paris was open, Philip did not take it. This was his first experience of war and he was not, by temperament, the man to stake everything on one crucial throw. Meanwhile the French called back from Italy the only soldier in Europe whose temperament and daring would have taken such a risk—the Guise. Once at the head of the French army, the Guise forced Philip to fall back again toward Flanders; and, having made a great muster of men round Amiens and Abbeville, let it be known that he intended to carry the war into the Low Countries.

That was not, however, his real intention. He had determined, at mid-winter and when least expected, to move north toward Calais, once he had convinced Philip and Savoy, by feints and forced marches, that he was driving eastward. Such a plan, of course, could not be kept entirely secret. Giovanni Michiel, the one-time Venetian Ambassador to England who was now in France, heard rumors and reported it. Wentworth himself became alarmed by the stories brought to him of a long procession of carts, laden with powder and shot, battering and field guns, ladders, planks and horsemen moving mysteriously through the long nights. On Christmas Eve, he wrote to the Lords of the Council of his fears of an attack, explaining that he could not defend Calais but, while abandoning the town, would try to keep the turnpike.

Mary furiously reproached him with cowardice that "being in such a place he stood in fear of his own shadow" and Philip offered to come at once to reinforce him. But Wentworth, even if he had been a brave and enthusiastic commander, had difficulties enough. When he tried to organize the defenders, he found that "the women did more labour about the ramparts than the countrymen who did absent themselves in houses and other secret places." On the other hand, there was no lack of organization among the English traitors who, on the eve of Guise's attack, escaped to the French and gave them every detail of the defense.

On New Year's Eve, Guise made the first attack on the countryside to the northwest of the town. On January 6, the French, after an interim of gallant and bitter fighting on the outskirts, took the castle of Calais without a blow. Next day Wentworth surrendered. Had he held out one day more, Philip would have relieved him, though, even without the arrival of a relieving army, Guise would have been forced to retreat by the hurricane gales which, while they impeded the arrival of English shipping, were equally endangering the French supply line.

So Calais was lost—"by negligence of the Council at home, conspiracy of traitors elsewhere, and force of enemies, helped by the rage of the most terrible of tempests." On the very day that the news reached England—"the heaviest tidings that ever was heard of"—a great gale in the Channel, dismasting the English ships and driving them ashore, put an end to hope of a counter-attack. It was, some thought, as if it "was done by necromancy and the Devil was raised up and become French."

Mary fell into a profound melancholy. That the war could not be allowed to end until Calais was retaken was even less to her than the final revelation of that treachery which would never cease to harass her until it had killed her and destroyed her religion. Now all her people would have reason to abhor her name. She told her women that, if they opened her heart, they would find "Calais" written there as the cause of its breaking.

One hope only remained. She was, she was certain, pregnant again.

When Philip received the news of this, he sent his friend, the Count de Feria, to congratulate her, to estimate whether it was true, to report the temper of England and, with the utmost discretion, to discover whether Elizabeth would consider him as a suitor for her hand should Mary die.

Before de Feria arrived, Guisnes, the last fort in the Calais Pale, had fallen.

# TWENTY

# De Feria
# Reports

*Extracts from the letters of the Count de Feria to King Philip*

London, February 2, 1558

I arrived here on Wednesday afternoon, January 27. I might have arrived earlier, but loitered on the way so as not to bring with me the news of the fall of Guisnes, which accompanied me across the Channel. I went to kiss the Queen's hand and gave her Your Majesty's letter and good news of your health, which she received with great pleasure. It would be well if all those who govern the kingdom shared the Queen's spirit. She told me that on the following day she would summon the members of the Council so that I might address them. She could not do so earlier because in the morning they were busy with Parliament.

I urged them to make haste to get as many ships as possible out for the defence of their coast. They are so fearful and downcast that if a hundred men landed in England they would not put up any resistance and might actually turn against their friends.

I am told that since the fall of Calais not one-third as many Englishmen go to Mass as went before.

London, February 12, 1558

Plenty of rumours are running about London every day, mostly unfavourable to us. Among other things they are saying that I have come to carry away money to Your Majesty. I shall be content if I can induce the English to raise for themselves the money they so badly need. The Queen is very pleased with the amount that has been voted by Parliament and with the goodwill displayed. But it seems to me very little, considering the needs of the kingdom, and I have told her so, begging her to devise means for obtaining more, because otherwise both she and the country will be in grave peril. Cardinal Pole and members of the Privy Council have again and again said the same to me. They all stick to it that the grant is the largest that has ever been voted to any king of England.

Your Majesty should write to the Queen, because that would mean more to her than anything else, and I will keep at work on her at this end. Everything these people do is confusion and hatred, one against another. Whatever they decide one day, they undo the next.

At Dunkirk there is not as good a supply of vessels for the Channel crossing as there ought to be. The Queen thinks it would be well to have men-of-war there for this purpose. All I know about it is that the captain of the port is a fellow who in a very leisurely manner advises you to board some pumpkin and then stands on shore looking at you as if you were on the best ship in the world.

Parliament has been prorogued, not dissolved, because the Queen considers that the persons sent to it have transacted business so well and with so much goodwill that these same persons had better be summoned when Parliament meets again.

London, March 10, 1558

I am at my wits' end with the Council here, as God is my witness, and I do not know what to do. Your Majesty must realise that from night to morning and morning to night they change everything they have decided and it is impossible to make them see what a state they are in, although it is the worst any country has ever fallen into. If it were only a question of them, I think the best thing to do would be to let them get into the power of anyone who might take them over, for that is what they deserve. But I am afraid they might drag us after them. The Queen tells me she is doing all she can. She certainly has spirit and goodwill. With the rest it is hard labour.

The Council has so many members that it seems that no one has been left out, except William Howard, who was formerly Admiral; and numbers cause great confusion. They do nothing but raise difficulties, whatever one proposes, and never find any remedy. I warned the Queen of the danger to her person and the kingdom of these incompetent Councillors who all say that the country is rich and then add that they do not know how to raise the necessary money to defend it and recover its lost reputation.

I emphasized this point as much as I could while enlightening her as to the truth. She had not been entirely informed of how badly the English troops had done in Your

187

Majesty's army last year, nor had she been disabused about the story that it was they who had got first into St. Quentin. And when I enlightened her, incidentally, she was very distressed.

She is going to Greenwich today, nobody having been able to prevail upon her to put off her departure. The one thing that matters to her is that Your Majesty should come to her. It seems to me that her pregnancy is only something that she is determined to make herself believe, though, of course, she could not admit it.

### Greenwich, April 6, 1558

Since I arrived here on March 20, we have seen no letter from Your Majesty, although there have been letters from Court, dated March 27 and 28 reporting that Your Majesty was well. God be thanked! The Queen has been somewhat reassured by these news. She told me to write by this courier and tell Your Majesty that she is not writing because she is waiting for a reply and also because she is very much taken up with Holy Week ceremonies.

### Greenwich, May 1, 1558

The Queen has been looking forward to the arrival of the courier announced in your letter. She is somewhat better than she was a few days ago, but she sleeps badly, is weak and suffers from melancholy; and her indisposition results in business being handled more slowly than need be.

An ambassador of the King of Sweden came here recently. Several days passed without his having audience of the Queen or even demanding it. His mission appears to consist of two parts: one about commercial affairs between

England and Sweden, and the other to negotiate a match between the Lady Elizabeth and the King of Sweden's son, for which purpose he brought a letter from the young man accrediting him to the Lady.

Before he had been received by the Queen, he went to present his letter to the Lady Elizabeth! The Queen is writing to you on the subject.

When the Ambassador first arrived, the Queen was greatly distressed, thinking that Your Majesty would blame her because the match proposed a year ago for the Duke of Savoy had not come off. Now that the Lady Elizabeth has answered that she does not wish to marry, the Queen has calmed down; but she takes a most passionate interest in the affair. She now realizes that her pregnancy has come to nothing and seems afraid Your Majesty will urge her to take a decision about marrying off Elizabeth. I think Your Majesty ought to do this, grasping the occasion supplied by this ambassador and the pregnancy matter. I do not think the Queen will now wish to prevent Elizabeth from succeeding, in case God grants no issue to Your Majesties.

London, May 18, 1558

I have received Your Majesty's letter which arrived on May 16. The Queen has taken patiently Your Majesty's decision not to come for the present. Indeed, it was clear to everyone that it would not have been reasonable to expect you to come at this time. However, Her Majesty had given orders that the fleet should be ready at Dunkirk and Dover and lodgings prepared for you between the coast and London. She is suffering from her usual ailments. Yesterday she decided to come to St. James's Palace. She

189

came by land to Lambeth, in one of the heaviest rainstorms ever seen.

I did not see the Lady Elizabeth when she was here. As my principal support in negotiating those matters I was sent here for was the Queens' goodwill, I thought I had better avoid upsetting her. I afterwards sent to excuse myself to Elizabeth by the Admiral's wife, who was brought up with her and is devoted to her, telling her that since she left Town a courier arrived from Your Majesty instructing me to visit her on your behalf. I do not think that things ought to be left there, but that it would be well if I did go to see her before I leave the country. She lives about twenty miles from here. If I am to see her, you must write to the Queen.

English affairs are certainly not as they should be where Your Majesty's service is concerned. Every day that passes sees a turn for the worse. I am not at all satisfied with the Cardinal.

London, June 6, 1558

The courier Your Majesty sent on the 28th arrived on the 31st. After reading your instructions, I spoke with the Queen, who wished me to meet the Cardinal and her Council in her presence, and to address them. This I did. After discussion, the Treasurer was instructed to see to supplying provisions for the fleet so that it should be able to go to sea this month and continue to serve until the end of September.

When these people first made up their minds to form a large fleet, they assured me that they would be able to land as many as 10,000 men. Since then they have come down to 5,000. Now the Admiral seems to think he might land 7,000. As for me, the English never take me in, because I never believe a word they say. And, as I often check up on them, they find me tiresome.

If it had not been for their fear of the fleet the Hanseatic Towns were said to be forming, they would never have fitted out so many ships. Now, the whole kingdom is complaining of the expense involved and expressing doubts whether any useful purpose will be served by it. In order that they may not blame Your Majesty in this connection, I have taxed several Privy Councillors with the plain facts of the matter—that they would never have fitted this fleet out except to protect their own trading interests—and they have confessed that it is true. I have not spoken to the Queen about this, but I intend to do so before leaving, in order that they may not make her believe something else.

The Queen is not of the opinion that it would be well to reprove the Swedish Ambassador, in the presence of the whole Council, for having gone to see the Lady Elizabeth. She thinks it would be sufficient to have the Chancellor and the Treasurer present; and so she will proceed.

I am going to see the Lady Elizabeth on Friday, as Your Majesty has ordered me to do.*

London, June 23, 1558

Your Majesty's letter reached me on the 22nd and it was longed for because three weeks had passed without bringing any news of Your Majesty. Thank God, you have been well! The Queen is better than she has been recently. She had suffered from some of her customary ailments.

The Council are now in a different mood and are laying

* Philip, in his letter, had written: "I approve of your intention not to leave England without visiting the Lady Elizabeth. I am writing to the Queen that I have instructed you to do so and that she is to speak to you in the same sense. I hope that the Queen will take it well."

stress on the danger from Scotland. They have sent the Bishop of Ely and the Master of the Rolls to inspect the frontier and devise means for defending Berwick. Just the job for a bishop and a lawyer!

I went to visit the Lady Elizabeth, as Your Majesty instructed me to. She was very much pleased; and so was I for reasons I will tell you when I return.

London, July 5, 1558

A fortnight ago we had news over here of the loss of Thionville, and some of these Privy Councillors were highly delighted at it. Since then, people have been saying that Gravelines and Dunkirk have also been lost. I failed to find out where this rumour originated, but this afternoon it reached the Queen. She summoned me to Durham Place and told me that she wished to send off this messenger at once to find out what really happened. She says that the merchants of this kingdom will no longer dare to send their wool to Bruges, now they have heard these news. You cannot imagine what a state this kingdom has fallen into.

I discussed with the Queen a proposal to send the Admiral, with all the ships he has at Portsmouth and Dover, over at once. At that some of the Councillors began to say that they had heard that the French had taken Alderney and that the Admiral ought to sail in that direction, because Alderney was important. I did not dare to contradict them because, to tell Your Majesty the truth, I am afraid that if four French ships were to land men in England there would be a revolution here.

When the Queen reproved the Swedish Ambassador in the presence of the Chancellor and Treasurer for having

". . . certain she was dying . . ."

"Elizabeth had her Queenship . . . and snatched from it
what joy . . . allowed her."

made a proposal to the Lady Elizabeth without her knowledge, he put up a feeble defence, but then repeated his request. Her Majesty answered that she did not intend to proceed further in this matter . . .

A fortnight later, de Feria left England and rejoined King Philip and the Duke of Savoy at Mons.

# TWENTY-ONE

# Deathbeds

IN ESTRAMADURA, in the Hieronymite mon-
astery of Yuste, high on a mountainside lived, as a lay-
brother, the fifty-eight-year-old Charles who in the world
had been "King of the Romans, King of Germany, of
Castile, of Leon, of Aragon, of both Sicilies, of Jerusalem,
of Dalmatia, of Navarre, Granada, Toledo, Valencia,
Galicia and Mallorca, of Sardinia and Corsica, the Canary
Isles and the Indies, the Islands and Continent of the
ocean; Archduke of Austria; Duke of Burgundy, of Brabant, of Lorraine, of Styria, Carinthia and Krain, of Lux-
embourg, Limbourg, Athens and Patras; Count of Hapsburg, Flanders, Tyrol; Landgrave in Alsace; sovereign in
Asia and Africa." Each day, when he woke, his confessor came to pray with him. As soon as he was dressed,
he heard Mass either in his own room or in the monastery
chapel. At midday he broke his fast, during which he discussed historical and scientific subjects with those
schooled in them; but when the meal was over, and before he took his siesta, his confessor came once more to
read and discuss passages from St. Bernard or St. Augus-

195

tine. Three days a week, during the afternoon, he heard a special sermon and "never wearied, however long it might be." For Vespers and Benediction he attended chapel and sang with the monks. So, in this quiet daily rhythm, hidden from the world, he "made his soul." He had left the dead past to bury its dead when, arrived at last in Spain from Flanders, he had submitted his conscience, burdened with what he had done or been forced to do as Emperor, to five theologians and canonists and, after due penance, received absolution.

One August day, sitting on the terrace where he could look across the flower-filled garden and its fountains to the plain below with its forest of cedars, chestnuts and ancient oaks, he asked to be shown some of the paintings of Titian, his favorite artist who had made so many portraits of him and his house. At the *Last Judgment*, he was gazing long and intently when he started to shiver uncontrollably and was forced to admit to those around him that he felt unwell.

For three weeks, he lay ill of a fever, waiting for his end. During them, so single-minded was he in his thoughts of God, that his counselors and friends were awe-struck. He had already been anointed when the Bishop of Toledo arrived and, arriving, brought the tensions of the world into that atmosphere of simple and unquestioning faith. Charles was repeating the *De Profundis* when the Archbishop held out a crucifix saying: "Here is He who answers for all; there is no more sin; all is forgiven." Many of those present, knowing that the Archbishop during his travels abroad was suspected of having become tainted with heresy, saw this as an admission of his Protestant leanings to Luther's doctine of salvation by faith alone. Knowing the dying man's horror of heresy, they asked

196

the Archbishop to be silent and, in his place, a simple monk told simply the story of St. Matthew, whose feast day it was, and of St. Matthias, on whose day Charles had been born. In the guardianship of these apostles, the Emperor might find comfort on his last, uncharted journey.

Charles, who during his illness had never ceased to intercede for the peace and unity of the Church, said a last prayer for it: "Lord, into Thy hands I have commended Thy Church," sent his final remembrances to his son, Philip, and bringing to his lips his crucifix, which had belonged to Philip's mother, breathed his last word, "Jesus."

## II

Mary was at St. James's when news of Charles's death reached her. An intermittent fever, which she had caught at Richmond in the damp summer, was an illness added to the dropsy that had swollen her and the cancer that was consuming her. Though she herself refused to surrender, those about her were certain she was dying.

Her bodily sufferings, however, oppressed her less than her agony of spirit, as loss succeeded loss. The loss of Philip and of her hope of an heir might be an old pain, habituated by repetition; but the loss of Calais still had the sharpness of its first impact which was even increased by her gradual realization of the meaning of the treachery which had procured it. Now the loss of Charles outweighed them all, for with him went hope for her and for Christendom. An age was over; the centuries of faith were ended. Now that he could no longer come from Yuste, like one of the legendary heroes awakened by the world's need from their sleep in some hill-side cavern, she saw his greatness as it was. His mistakes were dwarfed by his achievement; his cruelties were necessities; his ambitions were seen to have been controlled by his devotion. Once, he and she might have checked the flood of chaos and heresy which was engulfing Europe. Now it was for ever too late. It was time for her to join him. At last she was content to abandon her will to death.

Philip, when he received from Mary's physicians a report on the dangerous condition into which she had fallen, sent de Feria again to England with instructions to secure from her at all costs before she died her nomination of Elizabeth as heir and her consent to her marriage to Savoy or "another of his choice." With de Feria traveled the best physician in Philip's dominions, a Portuguese, who, the King hoped, might at least be able to keep death at bay until all was decently concluded.

On October 28 Mary so far deferred to Philip's wishes as to add a codicil to the will she had made in March when she had thought she was pregnant. But even now she could not bring herself to name Elizabeth as successor. Her conscience and her courage still held and, by a last effort, she turned that formal document into an expression of love for her faithless husband that might speak to him from beyond the grave.

"Albeit that my most dear Lord and Husband shall, for default of an heir of my body, have no further rule within this realm, yet I most humbly beseech His Majesty, in recompense of the great love and humble duty that I have always borne unto him and for the great zeal and care which His Majesty hath always since our marriage professed and shown unto this realm, and, finally, as God shall reward him, I pray (I hope among the elect servants of God) that it may please him to shew himself as a father in his care, as a brother or member of this realm in his love and favour, and as a most assured and undoubted friend in his power and strength to my heir and successor and to this my country and the subjects of the same."

She bound her successor, whoever it might be, not only to pay her debts but to continue the Crown donations to the refounded religious houses and to carry into execution a new project which she might not have time to complete—the building and equipping of a hospital for wounded soldiers and sailors.

As she signed the codicil, her "Marye the Quene" was smaller than usual, showing signs of effort in the writing.

The following week, the Lords of the Council came to her bedside to make one last importunate attempt to persuade her to carry out Philip's wish and name Elizabeth as her heir. As she looked at the pitiless faces of the men whose greed and faithlessness had prevented the restoration of the religion they professed, she was reminded of hungry dogs . . . the dogs from whose mouths God had not yet delivered her. They, even more than the heretics, some of whom at least were honest, had defeated her. She saw this now with the clarity that comes with death and, seeing, struggled no more. Let them go to Elizabeth to tell her that she acknowledged her as her heir, provided that she remained firm and kept England firm in the Catholic faith which she now professed and practiced. But, even as she said it, she recognized its foolishness. Elizabeth, like Cranmer and Cecil and all their kind, would perjure themselves without a second thought. For them, the end had always justified the means.

After they had left her, the palace gradually emptied. All but her faithful and familiar friends joined the feverish procession to Hatfield to ingratiate themselves with her sister.

On Elizabeth their action made so great an impression

that she then and there resolved that, when she was Queen, come what might, she would never name an heir and would punish, even with death, anyone who suggested such a thing. She had, without their help, made all necessary arrangements through Cecil, whom she had appointed her Secretary. The only thing on which she was undecided was whether or not to marry Philip who, through de Feria, had again proposed it. Her mind was made up for her by the arrival of Robin Dudley, more magnificent than ever, on a white horse.

Mary, losing her frail hold on life, asked repeatedly for Pole. She could not understand his absence. Whoever in this world of treachery and time-serving might go to Hatfield, Reginald would not. On that she would be prepared to stake her salvation. They had to tell her that he, too, was dying and might reach the grave before she did. It was impossible for him to leave his bed at Lambeth. But when Pole realized her need of him he roused himself to write a last short letter and send it by the hand of his "ancient faithful chaplain," who was empowered to give and receive their last messages and farewells.

After this, she suffered spells of unconsciousness. Once her women thought she was gone, but she, coming to herself, comforted them and told them what good dreams she had had "seeing many little children, like angels, play before her, singing pleasing notes."

On November 17, she heard Mass very early in the morning. At the beginning, she was able to whisper the responses, but by the time of the Consecration, her power of speech had gone. As the Host was elevated, she raised her eyes in adoration, then bowed her head and did not raise it again.

## *III*

At Lambeth, when Mary's death was announced to Pole, he remained for a while in silent prayer for her soul. Then he turned to his friend Priuli, who recorded in a letter to his brother, the Doge of Venice, what followed: "He said to me that, throughout his life, nothing had given him greater content and happiness than the contemplation of God's overruling providence both in his own life and in those of others. He said that, in the course of the Queen's life and of his own, he had noticed a great similarity. She, like himself, had been harassed many years for the same cause and afterwards, when it had pleased God to call her to the throne, he had shared in all the other troubles entailed by that responsibility. He also pointed out their cousinship, the great similarity of their dispositions and the trust which they had in each other. He said that, quite apart from the immense mischief which might result from her death, he could not help feeling deep personal grief at it. Yet, by God's grace, the same faith in Divine providence which had always sustained him, consoled him still even in this final catastrophe.

"He uttered these words with such earnestness that it was evident that they came from his very heart and they even moved him to tears. He then remained silent for about a quarter of an hour; but though his spirit was great, the blow, having entered his heart, brought on the paroxysm earlier and with more intense cold than he had hitherto experienced, so that he said he felt it would be his last. He therefore desired that the book containing the prayers for the dying might be placed near him. He then had Vespers said as usual. This was about two hours before sunset, when he made his end so placidly that he seemed to sleep rather than to die, as had the Queen."

# TWENTY-TWO

# *Funeral Sermon*

THEY EMBALMED HER and took out her heart which, enclosed in a coffer covered with velvet and bound with silver, was buried separately in the Chapel of St. James's, where her body lay for three weeks in state. As she had asked, she was clothed there not in the royal robes of England, but as a poor *religieuse*. After death, the thorned crown had ceased its troubling.

The funeral, however, and all the outward trappings were royal enough and London, as the procession wound its way to Westminster Abbey, saw her once more in effigy, clothed in crimson velvet "with many gemmed rings on her hands." Had it not been for this, standing upright on the hearse as was the custom, men might have mistaken their first Queen-Regnant for a King. Before her went her armor—Chester Herald bearing the helmet, crest and mantle; Norroy the shield, the crown and the Garter; Clarencieux the sword; and Garter King-at-Arms the coat-armor. But the other four heralds—Somerset, Lan-

caster, Windsor and York—carried immediately in front
of the hearse banners of the saints. Imaged in embossed
gold on white silk, the Holy Trinity, Our Lady, St.
George and Mary Magdalene went before her to the
Abbey door where, on the indoor hearse awaiting her,
great waxen angels looked down on the coffin as it proceeded to the sanctuary. Here, all through the night, a
watch was kept by her own guard and "a hundred poor
men in good black gowns and hoods."

On the morrow the funeral sermon was preached by
John White, the Bishop of Winchester who had succeeded
Gardiner and who had been with her when she died. He
had, in Edward's reign, suffered imprisonment for the
Faith and was not given to compromise. Though aware
of the probable consequences, he had no intention of start-
ing to compromise now. Beneath his rounded periods was
a personal devotion.

He chose for his text a verse from *Ecclesiastes:* "I
praised the dead which are already dead more than the
living which are yet alive." He drew a picture of her:
"She was a King's daughter; she was a King's sister; she
was a King's wife. She was a Queen, and by the same title
a King also. She was sister to her that by the like title and
right is both King and Queen at this present of this realm.
What she suffered in each of these degrees before and since
she came to the Crown I will not chronicle. Only this I
say: howsoever it pleased God to will her patience to be
exercised in the world, she had in all estates the fear of
God in her heart. I verily believe the poorest creature in
all this city feared not God more than she did. She used
singular mercy towards offenders. She used much pity
and compassion towards the poor and oppressed. She
used clemency amongst her nobles. She restored more

noble houses decayed than ever did prince of this realm
. . ."

And speaking of "her rare devotion (praying so much,
as he affirmed, that her knees were hard with kneeling)
and of her grievous and patient death, he fell into such
an unfeigned weeping," says a chronicler, "that for a long
space he could not speak."

Gaining control of himself, he continued: "But although she were such a one, yet could she not be immortal.
It pleased God, in Whose hands the heart and breath, the
life and death, the beginning and ending of princes is, to
call her from this mortal life, of the pleasures whereof (the
pleasure she took in the service of God only excepted) as
no person here, I suppose, took less, so of troubles and
bitterness of the same, none here, for his estate, tasted
more."

The mere panegyric on her sister was sufficiently dis-
pleasing to Elizabeth, but the Bishop's conclusion threw
her into such a fury that, after it, she ordered his arrest
and deprivation of his bishopric. Nor, perhaps, in this
case, was the new Queen altogether without some show
of excuse. White reminded his hearers that Mary had left
a sister, Elizabeth, whom they were now bound to obey,
since a live dog was more effective than a dead lion. "I
hope she shall reign well and prosperously over us," he
added, "but I must still say with my text: 'I have praised
the dead more than the living' for certain it is that Mary
hath chosen the better part."

At last the little body was lowered into the grave prepared for it on the north side of the chapel which her
grandfather, Henry VII, had built; and Garter King-of-
Arms said in a low voice: "Pray for the soul of the most
puissant and excellent Princess Mary, by the grace of God

late Queen of England, Spain, France, both the Sicilies, Jerusalem and Ireland, Archduchess of Austria, Duchess of Burgundy, Milan and Brabant, Countess of Flanders, Hapsburg and Tirol. Defender of the Faith."

Over her tomb, as over that of Reginald Cardinal Pole in his cathedral of Canterbury, Elizabeth ordained that no memorial was to be erected. But when, later in her reign, the altars in Westminster Abbey were torn down by the Protestants, the consecrated stones were carried and laid on Mary's grave.

In Brussels, at the same time as the funeral service in Westminster Abbey, Philip attended in state two requiems —one for the repose of the soul of his wife, Mary; the other for the repose of the soul of his father, Charles.

# *Epilogue*

ELIZABETH HAD her Queenship and snatched from it what joy William Cecil and his hunchback dwarf of a son, Robert, allowed her. It was little enough though her reign, blood-marked by the murder of rivals, martyrs, lovers, was forty-five years long. At the end of it, she waited in despair for death.

Still round her neck hung her useless talisman, a gold piece the size of a coin. It had been bequeathed to her by a Welsh woman who had lived to the age of 120 and, dying at last, had ordered it to be sent to her with the message that, so long as she wore it on her body, Death would not touch her. Though John Dee had approved its possible efficacy, the effect had been the reverse of what she had hoped. Within a fortnight she had fallen ill and sickened to lassitude. One night she saw her own body "exceedingly lean and fearful" in the bright flames of a fire. Unable to decide whether it was dream, vision or mere trick of the light in a mirror, she asked her attendants whether they were "wont to see sights in the night." They were not. Terrified, she had sent down to Mortlake for Dee and ordered him to cast her horoscope. As a result, he had warned her to beware of Whitehall and to move to one of her other palaces. She chose Richmond rather than Hampton Court or her beloved Greenwich. Now it had one inestimable advantage. It was less than a mile from Dee's occult library and the laboratory where he cast his strange spells and where once he had seen the spirit Uriel holding the Philosopher's Stone which gives perpetual youth.

In her journey to Richmond, she had asserted her continuing youth. On that cold, wet January day with a northeast gale making it the bitterest weather men remembered, she had insisted on wearing "summer-like garments." Furs were for old people. Cecil observed that "there is no contentment to a young mind in an old body" but no one dared thwart her. Nor, as far as anyone could see, did she take any harm by it. Her malaise was of another order.

At Richmond she still refused to go to bed. The French Ambassador noted that she "appeared in a manner insensible, not speaking above once in two or three hours and, at last, remained silent for four and twenty, holding her finger almost continually in her mouth, with her rayless eyes opened and fixed on the floor where she sat on cushions without rising or resting herself." Old Howard of Effingham, her Boleyn cousin, knelt beside her on the cushions and counseled her to go to bed. She roused herself to give an angry refusal, adding in explanation: "If you saw such things in your bed as I do in mine, you would not urge it."

Dwarf Cecil, who was standing by, coldly curious, asked if she saw any spirits. She turned on him. This, at least, was a realm in which his writ did not run. "Little man! Little man! I scorn to answer you such a question."

But when he had gone, she turned to her cousin and, shaking her head violently as a half-broken horse might to rid himself of the collar, said piteously: "I am tied with a chain of iron about my neck."

He reminded her of her courage. She did not explain that what ailed her was beyond the limits of natural virtue and that, as she saw it, devils held the other end of the chain; but with great sighs said merely: "I am tied, I am tied and the case is altered with me."

The atmosphere of the palace stank of the occult. One night a lady-in-waiting, having assured herself that the Queen was asleep, left the stifling room to take some air. Four rooms away she met Elizabeth. In great trepidation she started to excuse herself for her seeming dereliction of duty. The apparition vanished and the terrified woman, returning to the Privy Chamber, found the Queen asleep exactly as she had left her. Two other ladies-in-waiting discovered a playing card, the Queen of Hearts, with a nail driven through the forehead, fastened to the bottom of the royal chair in which the Queen would not sit. In great fear, they left it where it was "remembering that the like thing was used to the old Countess of Sussex and afterwards proved a witchcraft for which certain persons were hanged." . . .

Elizabeth could not break out of the imprisoning circle, for of her own will she had banished that Power which could have freed her and had barred herself against Its re-entry. Cecil sent ministers of her own church, led by the Archbishop of Canterbury, to give her what comfort they could, but "bidding them be packing," she shouted: "I am no atheist and I know full well that you are but hedge-priests."

209

*Epilogue*

It was the last flash of her intellect. No priest came to her or could come. She consented at last to go to her bed and lay there, without hope, till Death came to hand her to Judgment.

# A Note on History

N<small>O FULL</small> or accurate history of Queen
Mary's reign exists and it is improbable that one can ever be
written. Too many documents were destroyed by the leaders of the victorious Protestant party under Elizabeth; and
much material from official foreign sources is still inaccessible.
The Spanish State Papers relating to English affairs from
1554 to 1558 were calendared only in 1954 and, as far as I
know, this book is the first to make any extensive use of them.

I should perhaps explain, since I must not assume that readers of this story are necessarily historians, something of the
nature of these sources. The originals (and some copies) of
the State Papers of the various reigns are kept in the Public
Record Office. The "index," so to speak, to these vast collec-
tions is the Calendar, in which the nature of the document is
listed, and in some cases the document itself is printed in full,
though more often abstracts are made or only those parts of
it which the editor considers important are fully transcribed.
The printed Calendars are thus the intermediary between
the "history" which is found in specialized history books and
the actual manuscripts which are the proper documentary
sources. Most historians, except in specialized work, are content to work mainly from the Calendars, with occasional
references to documents in essential or controversial matters.

For Mary's reign, however, the Calendar of Domestic State

Papers does not print anything but a line or two describing what the document is. There are no transcripts and no abstracts. This means that only a student who has read the actual manuscripts can really have any idea of the reign. An example may, perhaps, make this handicap clearer. For the year 1555, the Venetian Calendar occupies 300 printed pages, the Spanish Calendar 124 (of smaller print and narrower margins), but the Domestic Calendar only 9½ pages. What is more, there are 334 documents in the Venetian section, 255 in the Spanish, but only 141 in the Domestic—a proportion which suggests that the vast amount of English material which should exist (outweighing the Venetian and the Spanish put together) has disappeared, leaving us to rely more and more on ambassadorial dispatches and other documents sent to Venice and Spain which were beyond William Cecil's power to tamper with. This suspicion is increased to a certainty when we find that there are only twenty-five English documents for the first six crucial months of Mary's reign preserved in the Public Record Office compared with 187 for the first six months of Elizabeth's.*

Probably more revealing than either the Venetian or the Spanish Calendars would be the French, since the intrigues

---

* No one who has studied the Domestic State Papers can doubt that all of them went through Cecil's hands as soon as he became Elizabeth's Secretary of State on Mary's death and that he weeded them out with great thoroughness. To take one instance only: in the month of July, 1556, (Chapter XVI) when the conspiracy was still being unraveled and Mary wrote her bitter letter of reproach to Emperor Charles V of Spain there are only seven documents. Three of them are letters exchanged between Edward Courtenay and Sir John and Lady Masone; the other four concern Cecil. One is a receipt for various moneys paid out since May; one is his saddler's bill; one is his tailor's bill; and one is a financial account from one of his agents. Again, the November of 1557 (the month before the taking of Calais) there are only four documents. Two consist of Cardinal Pole's expenses for the year—one is virtually a duplicate of the other—and the remaining two are private letters about a Christmas invitation from Sir Philip Hoby to Cecil. So one could go through the entire reign.

of the French at the English Court and their fostering of the
various plots are the political pivot of the reign. But no collec-
tion of documents drawn from French ambassadorial sources
has been published in England; and though Vertot printed
some letters of Ambassador de Noailles in France in the
eighteenth century, he included by no means all the documents existing in the *Bibliothèque Nationale*.

Even the inadequate supply of the French Ambassador's
letters ceases in June, 1557, on the declaration of war, so that
for the last fifteen months of Mary's reign, there is silence
from that quarter. And what is worse, in the October of 1557,
the Venetian Ambassador, Giovanni Michiel—best and most
detailed of official observers—was recalled.

In addition to the State Papers, there are two other published official sources, the *Acts of the Privy Council* and the
contents of the "Baga de Secretis" dealing with the treason
trials printed in the *Reports of the Deputy Keeper of the Public Records*. And there exist also, of course, on the other hand,
various private diaries, chronicles and letters without which
any record of the reign, however inadequate, would be
totally impossible.

Unfortunately, however, the source from which the story
of Mary has been mainly constructed, at least for popular
consumption, is a powerful and inaccurate piece of Protestant
propaganda, John Foxe's *Acts and Monuments* generally
known as Foxe's *Book of Martyrs*. The damage this has done
to the cause of truth is incalculable.

It is as if, today, an official history of the American scene
from 1954 to 1958 were to be written exclusively from Soviet
propaganda. That is a rough analogy of what has happened
to the accepted history of England from 1554 to 1558. As one
historian* has put it, "to obtain a clear view of the Marian
persecution is not at all easy: Foxe's *Book of Martyrs* like a
great mountain range lies between us and the facts." During

* W. Schenk, in *Reginald Pole, Cardinal of England*, New York:
Longmans, Green, 1950.

the time of the events Foxe narrates, he was not in England but was one of the manufacturers of anti-Catholic propaganda abroad. His story when published was immediately called in question by contemporaries who were on the spot and who "made no bones about calling Foxe a liar." His legends of cruelty and injustices are merely reports of the prisoners' own unchecked and uncorroborated accounts, embellished, in certain cases, by unscrupulous invention.

In the actual reporting of the trials, Foxe is probably "accurate" in that he refrains (since there were the official records to check his version by) from inventing things that were not there; but he has no scruple in suppressing things that were, especially when sedition is involved. According to the impartial article in the *Dictionary of National Biography*, Foxe was "neither scrupulous nor scholarly" and had "loose notions of literary morality." Yet the impact of his book, used for centuries as a basic history for Mary's reign, has been incalculable.

This false impression was reinforced by the work of J. A. Froude, whose history of Reformation times, written between 1856 and 1870, still remains, in spite of its tendentious inaccuracies, the basis of the popular conception of Mary's reign. Froude's integrity as an historian was summed up once for all by E. A. Freeman, a careful historian who was his contemporary, in a verdict which posterity has not basically challenged: "Mr. Froude stands alone as the one writer of any importance of whose writings one can say that on them any process of correction would be thrown away. The evil is inherent; it is inborn. It is not mere colouring; it is not mere mistaken inference; it is not mere mistakes in detail, however gross the carelessness or ignorance which they might imply. It is the substitution, through page after page, of one narrative for another—a substitution of a story which bears no likeness to the original story, except that the same actors appear in both. . . . History is a record of things which happened; what passes for history in the hands of Mr. Froude is a writing in which the things that really happened find no place and in which their place is taken by the airy children of Mr. Froude's imagination."

Despite this, Froude remains the source of school histories, buttressed by the powerful English group of anti-Catholic propagandists like H. R. Trevor-Roper, A. L. Rowse and remnants of the once influential Whig wing led by G. M. Trevelyan, the historical heir to and collateral descendant of the Macaulay who was to the Stuart period what Froude was to the Tudor. Consequently when this book appeared in England, reviewers, steeped in orthodoxy, made against me monotonous accusations of "bias," especially as regards my attitude to the Marian persecutions.

As even some readers in the United States, (where, at the moment, historical scholarship is higher than in England) may, by an overspill of Froudianism, wonder why I have placed so little emphasis on the "burnings," it may be well to develop the point. The answer, in short, is: because these loom large only in subsequent propaganda-history, based on Foxe through Froude, and not at all in contemporary feeling, which is the thing I am trying to recapture.

This, by all impartial writers, was recognized even in England at least as long ago as 1910, when, in an introduction to Froude's *Reign of Mary Tudor*, W. L. Williams wrote: "Why has her (Mary's) memory been covered through centuries with scorn and obloquy? Froude will have it that it was due to a national detestation of the crimes which were committed in the name of religion. Those who take a more detached view of history can find little evidence to support the assumption. The nation as a whole seemed to acquiesce in the persecution. The government was weak, there was no standing army and Mary, like all the Tudors, rested her authority on popular sanction. Parliament met regularly. It was not the submissive parliament of Henry VIII. It thwarted some of Mary's dearest projects . . . But it never remon-

215

strated against the persecution of Protestants. It cheerfully revived the old acts for the burning of Lollard heretics. Froude suggests that Englishmen were aghast at the use to which they were afterwards put. But though Parliament after Parliament had been summoned after the Smithfield fires had been lit, there was no sign of disapproval or condemnation. When Edward died, there was an instantaneous return to Catholicism. When Mary died, Elizabeth had to walk warily in bringing about innovations in religion."

In the 'twenties, Canon Charles Smyth, a Protestant historian, published a most valuable book, *Cranmer and the Reformation under Edward VI* (New York: Macmillan, 1926) in which he had no difficulty in showing that, of the men and women who suffered under Mary, all but ninety would have been executed by Archbishop Cranmer himself had Edward VI lived longer; for because they denied the cardinal principles of Christianity they were abhorrent to Protestant and Catholic alike. (Cranmer did, in fact, burn two of their leaders.) Of the ninety, many of the most eminent, including Cranmer himself, were indubitably guilty of high treason (for which the penalty was more cruel and lingering than the fire) and many of the rest can most truly be seen as victims of what has been called "the panic reply of a social and political order threatened by a force which seemed determined on nothing short of anarchy." This is the true contemporary perspective and this I have tried to keep. And while nothing can minimize the courage and integrity of anyone who is prepared to die for his beliefs, whatever those beliefs may be, it should not be forgotten that it was the orthodox Lutheran Protestants abroad who referred to the English Protestants as "the Devil's martyrs."

Cranmer's own death is here put, I believe for the first time, into its exact place in the pattern of the conspiracy (Chapter XV). In most histories "the martyrs" and "the plots" tend to be treated in two water-tight compartments and only by a careful cross-referencing of dates, which readers understandingly neglect to undertake, can the integral relationship of the one with the other be understood. Once the matter is seen as certain actions undertaken by certain people on certain days, it becomes inescapably clear that Cranmer's death was due to his connection with the conspiracy and his own final action to his realization that the plot was discovered. There is no reason to suppose that, in other circumstances, Cranmer would not have been reprieved according to custom, especially since, to put it at its lowest, it would have been policy for the Government to have let him live.

Another case where exactitude of time and circumstance is important for understanding is the meeting of Mary and Elizabeth at Hampton Court (Chapter XII). This has so often been used out of context by playwrights and costume-novelists that it is necessary to insist that Mary saw Elizabeth because she feared death in child-birth* during the next day or two and wished to safeguard her husband's position. It was not an isolated or irrelevant meeting at which Philip from curiosity concealed himself behind an arras. Nor, on Elizabeth's side, was her composure a characteristic display of courage. It was an attitude conditioned by the horoscope foretelling that she would succeed to the Throne which had been cast for her by Dr. Dee who, from that moment till her death, remained one of the major influences on her.

There remains the question of the parentage of Elizabeth. Whose daughter she was is not, for the purposes of this story,

---

* The recurring illness from which Mary suffered was secondary amenorrhea (the cessation of the menstrual cycle in a woman of child-bearing age) *see* Sir Frederick Madden's Introductory Memoir to *Privy Purse Expenses of the Princess Mary* (1831). This condition is often the result of some acute emotional shock such as the death of someone or a broken love affair or of an adrenal disorder. It is frequently accompanied by signs of virilism such as the growth of hair and a deepening of the voice. Obesity may develop which could be temporarily mistaken for pregnancy.

important. I have dealt with the matter objectively and at length and given the evidence in my *Enigmas of History*. That essay was part of the preparation for writing this book, for the first requisite for understanding Mary's attitude to Elizabeth was to know whether she thought of her as a sister or not. And in this (which is quite distinct from the question whether her belief was or was not in accord with the facts) there is no room for any genuine doubt. Mary believed that Elizabeth was not her father's daughter.

If I may quote from *Enigmas of History:* "It seems to me impossible to deny that, whoever Elizabeth's father may have been, Mary believed that he was Mark Smeaton, as she told Jane Dormer; and for this belief she had reasons which in her own mind, could not be shaken. Against her inclination, against her self-interest, against her love for her husband and against the cause of the religion that was so dear to her, she took the only course she considered compatible with 'that which held her conscience for four and twenty years.' What proof she had, we cannot know: but, judging by events, it seems to have convinced Philip when at last she told him of it."

Finally, to guard against misunderstanding, I must emphasize the limited scope of this book. It is neither a biography of Mary Tudor nor a history of her reign. It is an attempt to present the relationship between Mary and Elizabeth from the time when Elizabeth's first attempt to dethrone her sister had failed until Mary's death, four and one-half years later. This relationship seems to me to be important, because it conditions most of Mary's conduct and, in great measure, explains the reign as a whole.

This is not the place to restate my theory of history, which I have formulated on various occasions elsewhere. It may be sufficient, for those unaware of it, to repeat what I wrote in my *George Villiers, First Duke of Buckingham* twenty years ago: "Many will object that this biographical attitude to

*A Note on History*

history is sadly *démodé*. I know. But my difficulty is that the mere fact of studying history makes it very difficult to avoid. History is the relationship and interaction of characters or it is nothing. You can impose on it arbitrary forms and explain it by any number of theories, but the fact remains that events are determined, destinies of people shaped, and forms of government altered by men and women who, by birth or beauty or genius, are in a position to impose their will upon their fellows. This truth has been best summed up, perhaps, in the famous *mot:* 'It was not the Carthaginian army which crossed the Alps. It was Hannibal.' "

In the years between, I have experimented with several techniques in an attempt to get as near as possible to truth—the truth that Freeman expressed so simply in the passage I quoted earlier: "History is a record of things which happened"—by discovering the nature of the people to whom or through whom they happened. And here, in trying to understand "Bloody Mary" in her relationship to her sister, I have tried to use the simplest technique of all to lead the reader to a truer appreciation of the happenings of her reign.

HUGH ROSS WILLIAMSON

*London: October, 1958.*

# Index

# Index

# Index

# THE AUTHOR AND HIS BOOK

HUGH ROSS WILLIAMSON, *historian, theologian, playwright and novelist, was born January 2, 1901 in the town of Romsey, Hampshire, England. He was graduated in 1922 from the University of London, with a B.A. Honors degree in history, a subject which he has utilized in most of his writings. He taught school for a short time and in 1925 joined the editorial staff of the Yorkshire Post. Later he became drama critic for that newspaper. He has written a dozen plays since 1927. One,* Mr. Gladstone, *first produced in 1937, was banned by the censor for stage performance because of its political overtones, although it has been broadcast and televised. Unable to serve in World War II because of lameness, he turned to the Church of England, being a member of the clergy from 1943 to 1955, when he became a convert to Catholicism. A frequent contributor to the British networks, Mr. Williamson has also appeared in most of Britain's scholarly and popular magazines. Among his books are:* The Poetry of T. S. Eliot *(Hodder and Stoughton, 1932; Putnam's, 1933);* John Hampden *(Hodder and Stoughton, 1933);* Gods and Mortals in Love *(Country Life, 1935);* King James I *(Duckworth, 1935);* Who is for Liberty? *(Michael Joseph, 1939);* George Villiers, First Duke of Buckingham *(Duckworth, 1940);* A.D. 33 *(Collins, 1941);* Captain Thomas Schofield *(Collins, 1942);* Charles and Cromwell *(Duckworth, 1946);* The Story Without an End *(Mowbray, 1947; Morehouse, 1947);* Were You There? *(Mowbray, 1947);* The Arrow and the Sword *(Faber and Faber, 1947);* The Silver Bowl *(Michael Joseph, 1948);* Four Stuart Portraits *(Evans, 1949);* Sir Walter Raleigh *(Faber and Faber, 1951);* The Gunpowder Plot *(Faber and Faber, 1951);* The Seven Christian Virtues *(SCM Press, 1951);* Jeremy Taylor *(Dobson, 1952);* The Ancient Capital *(Muller, 1953);* Canterbury Cathedral *(Country Life, 1953; Transatlantic, 1953);* The Children's Book of British Saints *(Harrap, 1953);* The Children's Book of French Saints *(Harrap, 1954);* The Children's Book of Italian Saints *(Harrap, 1955);* The Great Prayer *(Collins, 1955; Macmillan, 1955);* Historical Whodunits *(Phoenix House, 1955; Macmillan, 1955);* James, By the Grace of God— *(Michael Joseph, 1955; Regnery, 1956);* The Children's Book of Spanish Saints *(Harrap, 1956);* The Walled Garden *(Autobiography; Michael Joseph, 1956; Macmillan, 1957);* Enigmas of History *(Michael Joseph, 1957; Macmillan, 1957);* The Day They Killed the King *(Muller, 1957; Macmillan, 1957);* The Beginning of the English Reformation *(Sheed and Ward, 1957);* The Mime of Bernadette *(Burns Oates & Washbourne, 1958);* The Challenge of Bernadette *(Burns Oates & Washbourne, 1958; Newman Press, 1958); and* The Children's Book of German Saints *(Harrap, 1958). Mr. Williamson is a cousin of the first Viscount Simon, foreign secretary and lord chancellor, and, like him, of Plantagenet descent through the martyr Blessed*

*Margaret Pole, the Countess of Salisbury. He is married to the former Margaret Joan Cox, a scientist who is a television producer in the Schools Department of the BBC; they have two children, Julia and Hugo, and make their home in London.*

THE CONSPIRATORS AND THE CROWN *(Hawthorn, 1959) was designed by Ernst Reichl and completely manufactured by George McKibbin & Son, Brooklyn N.Y. The body type is Linotype Janson, based on the letters of Anton Janson, a Dutch punchcutter who worked between 1660–1687.*

A HAWTHORN BOOK